Eiffel Tower

Texas Tree

ding

Christmas Tree Pins of the World

by Hanna Bernhard Paris
on
www.French-bakelite.com

Chinese Pagoda

Egyptian Pyramid

Oriental Hand

ISBN-13: 978- 1-4196-8703-7

ISBN-10: 1-4196-8703-4

Art Director *Tom Holzhauer*
Cover Design *Nathalie Bernhard*
Photography *Kathy Flood, Dennis Scheer*
Publication Reps *Bethany Snow Myers, April Bogdon*

COLLECTING

COSTUME

JEWELRY

CHRISTMAS

TREE

PINS

KATHY
FLOOD

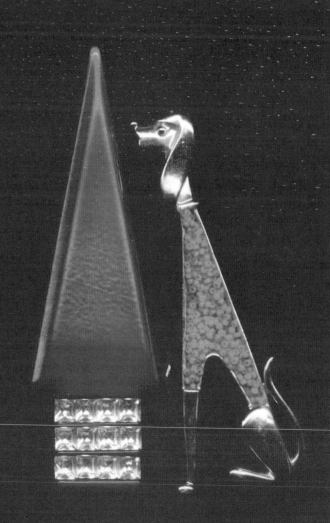

Dedication

For some of the friends who've made pin hunting in the forest so much fun over the past 15 years: Mary Watson Arroyo, Susan Radosti, Carol Stolworthy, Karen Parnella Workman, Jeannie Barnes, Celeste Dembowski, Marjorie Armstrong, Carolyn Short, Leah Luper, Fran Smith, Jennifer Flory, Denise Wedel, Neta Lovell, R.L. Smith, Elaine Simpson, Susan Gibson, Tamara DeFazio, Linda Kraus, Harriet Corn, Paula Beck, Judy DeVivo, Dee-Ellen Cook, Sherri Wells, Joanne Hobin, Judi Gerard, Charie Kerr, Pam Wood, Coral Oldfield, Karen Firmin, Betty Bartlett, Jackie Torngren, Sara Garson, Kay Shaw, Mary Lou Messick, Shirley Shier, Diana Todd Irish, Lynda Bagley, Helga Donohue, Nancy James, Anny Bate, Nancy Linke, Sharon Bembery, Sally Pisani, Sabina Vidunas, Carolyn Davidson, Ann Mitchell Pitman, Bobye Syverson, Patsy Seal, Barbara Wood, Joan Vogel Elias, Carol Spigner, Trish Lablonde duPond, and Peter Defabio.

On the Covers

If you possess the prickly jeweled porcupine tree by Jollé, you know how hard some marks are to locate. The first time I saw a Hanna Bernhard Paris brooch, I thought the jaw-dropping jewelry was unsigned. Collected as investment pieces by a growing cadre of international aficionados, Hanna Bernhard creations come out of the cosmopolitan capital of France. One hotbed of collecting passion for these Parisian works of art is Dallas, where I used to live.

Since volume one, which you hold in your hands, focuses on unsigned holiday brooches, it turned out *les Bernhards* belong instead in a signature book. But in the best European tradition, the French firm became the *patron* of the tome. They designed and produced an array of wildly unusual trees to bookend the pages, showcased here for a big *soupcon* of splash and statement.

The people behind Hanna Bernhard Paris are a married couple, Nathalie and Fernand, who may have been meant for each other, wedding distinct individual talents into one successful jewelry studio. Nathalie was weaned on art, handcrafts and jewelry, eventually becoming a collector, then designer, studying jewelry-making techniques in the 1980s. Fernand had the same passion for color – he grew up on Corsica – but was a dental-prostheses specialist by profession. They decided to tackle and explore the art, craft and techniques of making highly sculptural bijoux together.

Designing their first full collection in the early '90s for Fabrice, they made their first Christmas tree brooch in 1993. Each piece is one of a kind; most stones are vintage Swarovski crystal, old paste, glass elements and semi-precious stones. Some brooches enjoy special displays created to present the pieces, so collectors can enjoy the jewelry as decorative works of art when not wearing them.

With so many trees available on the jewelry market, Nathalie says they attempt to design highly unusual forms. "We also try to find things with shapes similar to trees, like the top of the Chrysler Building, and transform them into holiday motifs," she says. They feel many of the brooches are, *naturellement*, French looking, but also wanted to create an international lineup, including trees of the world representing, for instance, what they think an arbor from India might look like, were there one. "We like to travel and meet people," Nathalie notes, "so it is a way to just say we like people ... and to wish everyone 'peace on earth.'" The Hanna Bernhard Paris forest includes about 50 (and growing) different trees. Fans of figural jewelry can reach them at french-bakelite@noos.fr

Introduction

Collectors and historians alike appreciate accounts and anecdotes that illuminate their sometimes complicated subjects. Remember the scene in 1973's *The Paper Chase*, when Hart (Timothy Bottoms) takes his struggling friend Kevin (James Naughton) to see a law tutor? The legal whiz presents Kevin with a case or conundrum and tells him to figure it all out and when he does, he'll understand law. The clarity and illumination that scene promises tends to stick in one's mind.∑

One ah-ha moment came along while researching costume jewelry. In New York City, I met with Lianna's Paul Verrecchia one afternoon for interviews, and Mylu founder Marge Borofsky at her apartment later that same evening. They coincidentally and separately wound up showing me a partridge-in-pear tree pin (each identical to the other) that they claimed was 'theirs.' Since each person had been nothing but straight-shooting and honest, I sat there staring at Borofsky's brooch, trying to screw up my courage to ask what sounded like an insulting question. I queried as breezily as possible, 'Did you ever wind up using other people's designs?' The answer was short and sweet: No! Hmmm. I turned back to Verrecchia by phone, to chat about the pin. It was, he said, a vintage design from his father Alfeo's Gem-Craft archives, one he had brought back at Lianna.

Partridge

Mylu

Paul Verrecchia

And so all was clarified. Sisters Marge Borofsky and Lynne Gordon had their Mylu Christmas jewelry line made at Gem-Craft, where they worked closely with Alfeo Verrecchia and his team on designs. They may have had a sketch of a partridge tree, they may have had a detailed drawing. Alfeo and his model makers executed designs, tweaked them, and also designed jewelry from scratch. So the fact both people showed me that same pin as their own provenance was correct. Paul pulled it from his father's Gem-Craft archives, and Marge had her tree in her collection. It gives you a glimpse into how designs are born, move around, and live on to reappear another day.

But Marge and Paul also contributed to our understanding of why jewelry was or was not marked, which is of special interest here.

After Paul presented a dozen brilliant vintage Christmas tree designs from his dad's archives, I asked if any were marked with the Gem-Craft name, or with Alfeo's initials or … anything. Paul explained that since they made jewelry for other companies, whether a wholesaler such as Capri or a jewelry house such as Cadoro, the Gem-Craft name, with very rare exception, was not stamped on. Some of the Verrecchia designs are Christmas classics (see tem later in the book) but hadn't been attributed or credited (until now).

Contrast this with an entirely different situation at Mylu. Almost every single Christmas tree pin was marked (with one exception) Mylu – and later, Tancer II, Avante, etc. Marge was rigorous about their designs remaining theirs and being clearly identified as such. The story is legend in the costume jewelry world that when the Mylu sibs saw their own designs showing up in newspaper advertising for Coro, Marge quickly got Coro president Mike Tancer on the line and demanded a meeting. Tancer agreed, and reportedly when Borofsky showed up, Tancer broke out laughing that 'such a tiny thing stormed into my office to tell me off.' The jewelry business is infamous for borrowing designs, and since only a small change has to be made before a design is considered different enough to stand on its own, bitter feelings abound.

Tancer offered the sisters jobs soon thereafter, but they didn't immediately jump at the chance to become 'Mylu – a division of Coro.' Years later, after Tancer was fired, he founded his own eponymous jewelry company with the former Lewin sisters, known as Tancer-II.

Any near-twin vintage Mylu design you see unsigned is a copy, something that drove Borofsky nuts. Even when I met with her in 1999, she had spotted some copies of pins she made for K&M in a store and was considering pursuing legal action. What I wanted to know above all about marks was why Mylu's hard-to-find rivoli candles tree was sans signature. The answer was simple: she had no idea. As both Paul and Marge separately noted, it may have been forgotten; it may have been overlooked; the pin could have been a rush job; the pin may have been tagged … et cetera. It was never a big deal to anyone in the jewelry world, as it is to those of us who love and collect it. We crave knowing who did what.

Most of the vintage Mylu copies you find on the market don't hold a candle to the real thing. Mylu trees are brawny, buxom or bursting with good things, fully fleshed-out designs of quality manufactured by one of the best makers of all, Gem-Craft. The copies are scrawnier, lighter, more timid, and so clearly uninspired (except for the inspiration to rip off).

Even at Lianna, Verrecchia let many designs out of his jewelry house with no mark. I'd estimate fully a quarter to third of all Lia trees I've seen are unmarked. Paul Verrecchia was one of the talented designers I invited in 1999 to create a special tree for my book. When it arrived, uncannily, it was not signed.

Vintage Verrecchia

Alfeo Verrecchia and his Gem-Craft designers originated the sawtooth-edged trees shown here on top. The sawtoothed sapling in gunmetal with fuchsia and jewel-tone chaton on far right was reborn under Paul Verrecchia for Liannna, a lovely specimen itself. It's great fun to hunt for versions of this clever design. 1950s-99; $50-100. The three trees in center row are all old Gem-Crafts: with red bow, and the tree with dangling beads in its portholes, are also old Gem-Craft trees. The red-bow tree lives on and may be found in many permutations even today, but the original vintage version is the best. Look at the attention to detail, the many appealing elements, the wonderful use of crystals as ornaments. Don't you wonder which jewelry house Gem-Craft created it for? $50-100 for the vintage original. And the same can be said for the ingenious trees on left and right too, with unique star knob, inlaid gems studding the green ground … brilliant. Vintage versions, sometimes signed MV, are $50-150. The golden tree between two more unsigned sawtooths (bottom row) is fascinating because … one just like it was one of the earliest Christmas tree pins I ever purchased, in an Accessory Lady boutique, early Nineties. It was marked Lia. Many years later, I found this vintage unsigned version, with the same cut-out hearts, dangling beads and uniquely shaped tiers. Ah-ha: another old Gem-Craft tree, brought back to life decades later by Paul Verrecchia. This unsigned vintage version, $50-100.

This Is What The Hunt's All About

Christmas tree pin aficionados are spoiled rotten because at any time on any day, a vintage Christmas tree no one has ever laid eyes on previously ... may suddenly spring up. That factor is uncommon in the majority of collecting fields outside costume jewelry. The Christmas tree on the opposite page is a prime example of the phenomenon: a fabulous Fifties rarity that is exciting in its attributes - and scarce out of this world. I spotted it on eBay and had to have It. Few people seemed to notice the auction, but one eagle-eyed friend did. She regretted her high bid because it wasn't high enough. (She simply didn't think anyone else was watching.) My only concern before it arrived was that it might have originated as other than a brooch, that someone simply attached a pin mechanism to something else, such as an ornament. For purists, that's a no-no. But oh joy, its roots actually are as a piece of jewelry. The old c-clasp pin is imbedded into the back and covered with the same old flocky, coconut-like flakes as the rest of the arbor. The metal feels like dense tin, snow white with enameled paint. The large tree is inset with - get a load of them - multicolor anodized aluminum bells. They are the color of the aluminum tumblers many drank lemonade from on a shade-covered swing away from the hot summer sun at grandma's house. Remember how the droplets meandered down the sides like cool little streams? How novel that such a distinct summertime memory is transposed here in this pin to wintertime. Did Alcoa decide to show off its Color Craft line in miniature for the holidays one year, with a company pin premium? It's one of my all-time favorites. 1950s, $100-250, depending on how much someone wants it.

Confetti Blast on Black

Brightly colored confetti hard-plastic'd into a glossy black plastic large-scale tree replete with crazy cabochon in l'etoile, with faceted gems elsewhere. Yowza. How do I love this brooch? Let me count the ways: a wild design aesthetic; lollipop colors that pop against licorice black; well-made despite being cheapish; uncommonly kooky. 1970s; $150

Viva la Galalith

Nathalie Bernhard found these striking vintage Art Deco trees for me, in butterscotch and berrywine Galalith, accented with glittering old square cuts almost resembling glass blocks. From Paris, they were 'dead stock' from a shuttered French emporium. The trees' rich colors, paste bijoux, and unusual size (4-5/8 inches) make them collectible and wearable both, for the person who doesn't like what everyone else has. Chic alors! $150-250.

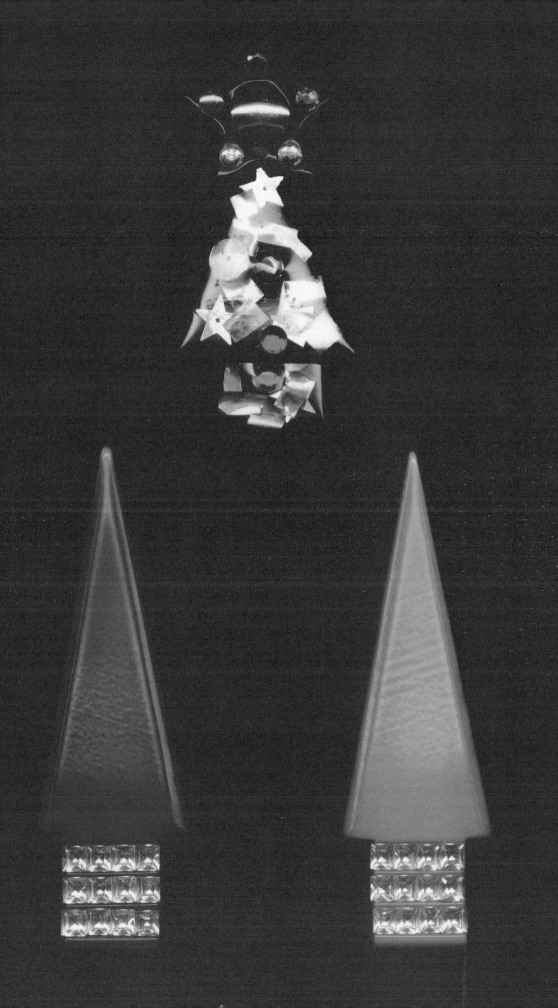

Blue, Blue Christmas

Growing up in a Catholic-Jewish neighborhood, I loved the exotic blue of Hanukkah decorating friends' homes. We had so little blue to do with Christmas, maybe that's another reason blue Christmas tree pins are exciting.

It's said most people claim blue as their favorite color. Holiday arbors are one place to indulge that aesthetic delight, since actually, we rarely indulge it anywhere else.

The pretty pale blue vintage tree on top (left) is a simple classic, unfussy and unimpeachable. I wrote a tree story through interviews with the daughter of a long-time Massachusetts Christmas pin collector who died. She had given trees to her closest friends, and every Dec. 24 at Midnight Mass they all wear them to honor Shirley. I purchased a few of the trees from Shirley Jr., and this was one of them. $25-50. Continuing across the top row, the fan-shaped fir that alternates pastel with pave presses all the right buttons in terms of fresh style and design. So feminine, it's contemporary and one of my favorites, $25-50. The elegant vintage tannenbaum next door is simple, but has a curious confidence, almost playful even in its tailored self. Pale turquoise beads sit modestly between simply scalloped tiers; $50+ The little masterpiece on far right is a gem, an unsigned Kramer creation with ridged, snow-tinged boughs of needles, a carelessly draped strand of blue lights coloring up the gray metal and mixing with cheerful pearls and the splash of color provided by a red-striped candy cane; $100-150.

A poor attempt to copy the great Dominique trees leads off the second row, flat but sure to jolt a *jupe* courtesy of all those royal-blue sapphire square cuts. Candles and dangles dress it up even more, while the tilted blue square-cut turned diamond on top is a nice touch; $25-50. Proof that new ways to design a Christmas tree pin are still out there, this 2006 tree stars blue-gray cough-drop beads hanging from metal bars like clothes lines with translucent accessories; $25-50+ depending on future availability. One of the many vintage rivoli trees (see pages 52-53), this particular one boasts blue-green tourmaline-effect glass beads, $50+. The tree of milk glass navettes mixed with sapphire and volcanic green marquis stones is one you'd expect to flip over and find the (fake) KJL cartouche, but this one doesn't even have that; $10-25.

Third row left begins with a puzzling pin, first featured as a Kenneth J. Lane product in the first Christmas jewelry book, by Jill Gallina. Because of that showcase, everyone wanted one. If you paid $75 for it, you were mighty surprised when it arrived, a piece of junk, unsigned (the one I bought, anyway), and looking unlike any other KJL work. It was a relief in a way to learn Lane had never designed even a single tree for his jewelry house; $25. The large tree with glassy mixed-size cabochons in blues and purples is contemporary and first cropped up ca. 2002; $25-50. Right is a wonderful vintage pin with add-ons that made it a tree. White enameling sets off the brilliant blue glass squares that look like little gifts; $50+

The vintage tree of diagonally arranged turquoise and forest green enamels gains interest due to metal swirls and thin rows of tiny green chaton; $25. Final three in lowest row are all upside-down dress clips, perfect for an antique jewelry accent at Christmas, worn through a buttonhole or on cuffs. The first two are pretty pastel florals; $10-25. The third is spectacular, an antique European clip festooned with Easter-egg colored hollow glass domes, topped with fuchsia paste petals, $75-150. Christmas tree clips are rare, so if someone advertises one, ask if seller is showing it upside down.

Silver Thrills

For fanciers of the black fashion statement, the silver Christmas tree pin is *de riguer*, for nothing looks so smashing against noir as chilly argent.

The unsigned silver pine is easy to find, and the forest of white metallics here is witness to that fact. The perfect note of oomph on a black turtleneck, or dressy holiday note on faux black fox, the silver tree is a dagger through the heart of dull.

Silvery siblings flanking the ends of top row admittedly have been done to death, in many permutations, but there is one in every collection because the chatons in ropy-wreathed settings sparkle – and look sweet set off with pretty bows; $10-25. The open-work tree (second from left) is terrific in person, with its hint of Deco, echo of Nouveau, and its steely-silver look that's sort of 'dressy industrial.' It's got curve and body, convexity and charisma; $50+ The solid sparkler to its right is most notable for the kooky, misshapen star we'd love to know if intentional – or accidentally cast that way; $25-50.

While looking at the tree of hearts in the second row, it would be instructive to include its related arbors in the bottom row. All of them make glitter look good. Who knew cheap glitter could be used to such great effect? All the trees in low row, plus the hearts tree, came from Value City and SteinMart years ago, each featuring a competent design, with glitter thrown on for sparkle. And it works. All of the designs are pleasing, and whether solid, gritty silver or with gold, they illustrate just how successful a tree can be at a very basic level; $25-50.

In the middle of second row, the tree of foliate flora could have been done up in red, but the manufacturer or designer went with straight silver; $10-25. The swirly sap of satin silver might be perfect for someone whose name commences with the letter 'C,' since they resemble it. This is a tree of very recent manufacture; $10-25.

In the third row: Diagonals are always a little different, and so is the strong mixed use of varying size crystals, lending the tree a bubbly effect. We could call it the Champagne tree; $25. Cold silver with imbedded crystals works well too, unimpeachable for its effective design simplicity; $25. Third, we all recognize this ruffled pine, an unsigned knockoff of the original vintage Lisner. The real Lisner is a gorgeous thing, this one not so much, and it is tarnishing like mad; $10. Finally, on right, the loopy lovely of wreaths with AB stones is actually Thai sterling, and came from Marshall's before the chain stopped carrying jewelry; $50

Unsigned? Who Cares?

Would you rather have a bad Weiss or a fascinating unsigned tree? If the latter, here are markless marvels that do a collection proud, signature or not. Moving left to right:

Top row: Vintage emeralds beauty didn't photograph well. In person it's lovely, has a certain *je ne sais quoi*, came on its original card, an ornament-shaped cardboard round marked Noel; $50+ Trembler Dove tree is one all collectors want because it's uncommon; few tremblers exist, and the bird of peace is crisply white against green; $50-100. One of the oldest topiary trees known, small but sweet, missing a few topaz berries and pea-green enameling. Poinsettias ball topped with star is scarce and unique; $50+ Holly-leaves tree of frosted Lucite enjoys unique style; soft green studded with hard, opaque red berry beads; $50+ Finally, one of two unsigned 'Chrysler Building' trees. From mid-90s, it's a cobalt-blue cabs confection with faux pearls and deco-atomic modernism. Originally available with cabs in any of five hues. One dealer, since disappeared, was the only one who had them and wouldn't say from where they came; $50-100.

Second row: A simple, vintage, razor-sharp design by Kramer, sometimes tagged. Its edges and geometric flat base give it an aesthetic with integrity. Also very well-made and cast; $50-100. More vintage simplicity in the second tree, subtle gold metal bezel-set with imbedded crystals, both brilliants and marquis, pretty and tailored, $50-100. Surely the great bronze beauty is a Beatrix, since the identical motif in candle and wreath pins are signed with that mark. The dramatic finish, exceptional casting, dimension, extras such as bells, candles and high-quality RS hues make it one of the great holiday brooches, $75-150. Far right is a vintage pin perhaps not worthy of fuss, but has detailed casting and metallic-painted molded ball ornaments, plus a nice little trunk; $25-50.

Third row: Layered fir purchased from Jill Gallina when she sold trees from the seminal book on Christmas jewelry. Textured metal tree gets glammed thanks to ruby rhinestone chain. It's a favorite. Who knows why? $75-100, partially because of provenance. Ultramodern vintage 'Aerial' tree, extremely abstract, hung with prong-set navettes and sleek baguette candles, $75-100. Right, vintage pin appears to have been cut from some fantasy glitter tree, with sparkle as well as nubby, wood-like bark, $50+

Fourth row: Perfect, tailored vintage tree, *soignee* boughs with detailed striations handsomely shaped and hung with faceted glass beads in jewel tones. Probably Kramer or Castlecliff; $75-125. Newer tree with refined details and twist on the expected poinsettia colors: green RS instead; $25+ Superb vintage tree boasts glassy rainbow of princess-cut crystals framed within iced-cookie tree shape, creamy enamel sweet and French Provincial; $100-150. Irresistible new tree with vivid color statement. Opaque snow-white epoxy mixed with glitter for grainy finish, decorated with dazzling RS and sparkling pot; $25+

Fifth row (random white remains): Semi-translucent plastic resin tree, painted gold tinsel and star, cellophane-ruffles effect; $25. Desirable vintage pine with cast faux ivory dotted in colorful crystals, fit into golden metal frame; $50-100. Small vintage tree done in creamy enameling contrasting with deep red star and tiny ornamentation; $25. Reproduction of a Weiss tree done in glittered epoxy, silvery metal crisscrosses bringing a drum-like effect. Cheaply made but appealing for its Weiss connection and scarcity. First appeared mid-90s; $50+.

Motifs Make Merry

Christmas tree pins that most tickle collectors' collective fancy could be the ones that incorporate icons into the tree or compose the arbor entirely. The top row illustrates both techniques perfectly, using one of the most popular holiday symbols of all, the angel.

Legions of Christmas tree pins completely made of angels stacked atop each other fly off jewelry counters every year. Some, such as the pearly, coveted Mary Beth for Pell design, are signed; most are not, as here (top left and right). The heavenly beings are dressed in pale blue, with drooping silver wings, or in glittery green gowns with gold wings that make seraphim look like scarecrows. $10 each. In the center is a favorite fir, purchased in a small shop along Main Street in old St. Charles: white-winged angels in colorful raiment blow their horns, tidings announcing (according to the heraldic banners) Peace, Joy and Love. The almost folkloric tree is practically gooey with thick, glossy epoxy, topping off with a heart-centered star. Its primitive paints are eye-catching. I found two, bought them both, and that was it. If this brooch remains scarce, $50-100.

In 2005, the Irish Christmas tree of silvery shamrocks was by far the best-selling pine in my shop, a green theme that graces many trees, but this one proved most popular; $50. (I think it's an import from Eire.) Isn't the Spoonful of Christmas pin delicious? I'm not sure I get it, but it always makes me want plum pudding. The utensil decorated for the holidays was actually manufactured this way. It's sort of cheapity-cheap, but novel and scarce, so $25-50. Gingerbread people are another staple of Yuletide fantasy, some spruces entirely shaped by stacks of cookie folk. Here we have two fat gingerbread revelers flanking a gaily glossed Christmas tree, large and heavy; $25.

If the vividly tinted, ribbon-draped stack of Christmas cookie tins on the left actually represents a tree, it may be the most creative construction ever; $25-50. The Teddy Bear tree is immensely popular and a bear to replace, so if you have one, hold onto it. It looks like a Lia piece, but is unsigned; $25-50. The golden pine of dollar signs, tsk-tsk, is what we like to call the Trump Tree. You can also wear it as a reminder of future credit-card bills when out Christmas shopping. Boy, that's a buzz kill. $25+

The tree hung with jeweled bells has an old-fashioned sensibility with its somber metal tone but romantic colors. Bells and candles may be the best add-on motifs of all when it comes to stylish Scottish pine pins; $50+ Feline themes are also wildly popular accompaniments to December's arbors. The number of Christmas tree pins with kitty wit is huge. Here, a trio of quizzical cats peek out from behind branches bedecked with red squares; $50+ Just above it (right) is the perfect Christmas in July motif, a beach lover's dream of pastel shells on a tree topped with – what else? – a starfish. $25

Beyond Poinsettias

Christmas tree pins composed of flowers are frequently memorable. Jewelry lovers have long liked floral brooches anyway, so it's no surprise holiday pines covered with flora never fall out of favor. The flowery firs the late Ian St-Gielar created were probably the ultimate in blooming Yuletide brooches, but even humble, no-name petal-covered Christmas tree pins are desirable.

Left to right: The golden flower garland of the first arbor features folded petals, which, combined with the open setting, give the tree integrity in detail. Large polychrome rhinestones lend color cheer to the mix, while a gritty pave trunk and sparkling crystal teardrop topper bring icy finishing touches. It's not old (late '90s-early '00s); $25-50. Flat, enameled vintage flowering tree isn't actually a tannenbaum, but the triangular shape allows it to be adopted into the fold; $25. Leafy-greens tree with red poinsettia accent has enjoyed a long life, first as a vintage incarnation but once again being made today. Its fresh design heightens its popularity; $50. And on top lower right, a tree of flowers different with its purple rhinestone centers clashing well with petals tipped in translucent epoxy. Collectors always appreciate a pot that's not an afterthought, so the emerald RS in a fancy basket-style bucket are a clever addition; $25-50.

Second row: Don't you love this? Some savvy observer of the tree scene co-opted an Ian St-Gielar design, one of his elaborate poinsettia pines dripping with beads and paste, and reduced it to an altogether wonderful budget lookalike. It's no Hagler or Gielar, but gets an 'A' for inventiveness using a gold-plated casting, some crystals, lots of deep-red epoxy, and those zingy star streamers. It's fun to collect copies of originals you love, so this might be a must for Hagler and St-Gielar tree fans; $50+ The center and right trees both look like Gale & Friends firs but are not signed. The silvery daisies pine is tremendously appealing for many reasons: spiky petals, sapphire baguette trunk, RS tinsel, and stars all over; $50+ The crystal cabochons tree is a kick when you first find one, glassy igloos covering trios of scarlet poppies, all draped with laurel-leaf wreaths; $50+

Third row: Up sprang trees of molded metal roses during holidays 1998 in department stores. Here are the three varieties of rose blooms grown that year: Roses d'or are simple, glowing, and appear to be bursting from a trellis; the silver roses have grown more interesting over time, as they have tarnished during the decade; and finally, the roses on right feel like stiffy flowers via sprayed netting, but could simply be a porous resin; $25-50+

Holiday Tree Houses

This is a terrific motif, part of the broad 'tree-with' category (i.e., tree with Santa, tree with snowman, tree with child) and a particularly charming one. There's something about a house or inn with Christmas trees that evokes memories of all the holidays we toured around and looked at such sites. The Lucinda House pins, which have many different Christmas trees as part of their design, aren't shown here because they are signed or carded.

The lighthouse with snow-laden pines and a single deer is perfect for someone with a home near water. It is from the 21st Century, $25-50. Is the silvery 'Peace on Earth' pin with Star of Bethlehem meant to represent the inns where Joseph and Mary reportedly could not score a room? That's what it looks like; maybe the stable's behind the buildings. Slightly older, 1980-90s, $25-50. The cheerful house with snowflake dangles has a lot going on around its cheerful façade: a snowman, a sled parked on the path, smoke curling out of the chimney and a heart smack on the house; 1990s, $25. The large golden cottage at center possesses particular appeal, perhaps because of the snow drifts piled up on the detailed building, or the contrast of gold and green, the dimensional casting, the open door revealing another tree inside; 1980-90, $75-100. Another cute cottage, bottom left, is festive in its red epoxy, wreathed door and snowy fir; 1990s, $25. An old-fashioned scene is extremely effective in recalling old times, with a couple in sleigh, merrily decorated Christmas tree, and a vine-covered abode with jeweled roof and red chimney. Looks absolutely vintage, but isn't. 21st Century, $25-50. A mill town setting is the subject of the rustic resin pin on bottom of page, with both a vague Tudor look and a watermill, 2002, $25.

Golden Find

A rare Christmas tree pin parure of 10k gold with simulated and semi-precious stones. The pieces include brooch, pierced earrings with star tops, and a large ring. As sweet as the suite is, it has a bittersweet backstory: a fellow had the group made by a jeweler for his sweetheart at Christmas. Years later, when she fell on hard times, she had to sell the set for cash. The dealer who sold the parure to me said she didn't know any more than that, whether the couple had remained together or not. The original box the pieces came in still holds the jewelry, and the card he wrote to her says,

"To Anne

Garnet

Chupprace (sic)

Sapphire

Rubi

Cats Eye

Citrine

Spinel

Zircon

Merry Christmas"

His signature and message are cut off; only the top loops of the letters are visible.

The pieces are well-made and executed. Hosting each polychrome, prong-set faceted stone on the branches is what appears appropriately to be an upside-down heart of gold filigree. The stylized trunks on brooch and earrings are striated to nice effect. The ring is a 3-D tree-shaped bush with an enormous shank. The earrings are slightly smaller than the brooch, or more compact, but are taller than the pin when the stone-set star tops from which they dangle are taken into account. The delicate filigree-heart branches contrast successfully with formidable trunks. The age is difficult to determine - perhaps 1970s or 1980s, although could be older; $500+

What Color is Your Christmas Tree?

Remember the first time you saw a pink Christmas tree in someone's living room? Chances are the owners also owned a poodle and vacationed in Miami. That's how exotic all those things seemed, back in the day. The very notion of pastel pink for a tree bordered on sacrilegious, till you realized how coolly kitschy it really was. Once you contemplate a rainbow, no single color will ever satisfy again.

In the world of holiday jewelry, what color hasn't been done? Hedison gets cred for its black arbor from practically ancient history. Lea Stein did it too, layered, with glossy white pinstripes. As for blues, purples and even orange, they've all been used to express the personality of a tree brooch. Offbeat chromes no longer shock from their perches on lapels.

Perhaps none are prettier than pinks. Look what the shade does for one of the homeliest Christmas tree pins ever designed (toward outside lower left). Whether you refer to it in the vernacular as the 'weeds tree' or the 'lilypads tree,' the usually tired old Gerry's design (maybe the most manufactured pine ever made?) gets positively glamorous with all that rose makeup. A pale splash of pink plus louder orangey rose are dressed up with pastel crystals and treated to a spring-green trunk. What's not to like about this contemporary tree in which pink turns a total drudge into a diva? $25-50 (depending on whether it continues being made)

The original Preppies knew nothing went with lemonade pink like a twist of lime, which is why we added that tone into the rosy mix here. Those hues, even separately, are delicious, but we've worn both the glittering trees (top left and right) together. They are two of the toniest tannenbaums recently made, hosting sparkling, layered navettes rimmed with pave-set brilliants, their dreamy 3-D dimensionality encrusted with gemmy splendor. And the trunk details are marvelous. Bargains at $50 each.

Below them (on left), green and pink cabochons mix it up for even more Preppy hijinx in a green-enameled rope-twist setting. This vintage design is sometimes signed Don-Lin, sometimes LJM. This version is our favorite. $50+

Dusty-rose on the skeletal vintage skirt-hoops tree (top center) is an accomplished enameling job. It looks interesting with the slightly clashing fuchsia stones. Those cold notes of silver at the joints bring a hard, modern edge to an otherwise feminine confection and build interest in its design, echoing the star and trunk; $50+

The circles tree (middle row, right) is a favorite because ... I fell for circle trees one year. There are lots of them, many vintage. This one's new, but fairly fetching with its stones pronged into open spaces within the pave-set circlets. $25-50. Below it (right) is a poorly made crafts tree I was duped by early on in my career as a forest ranger. It's a rather crummy creation, but photogenic; $10-20. Next to it (center) glow old pink-tinted faux moonstones, a brooch that lets you love Christmas without saying so too loudly. $25-50. And finally (bottom left), a small pale-rose rhinestone tree with openwork design, $10-20.

Serendipity in Blue

In St. Louis, off Jefferson Avenue, Cherokee Street runs for blocks with dozens of antique shops lining the little boulevard. It's the kind of destination that holds promise because it is suitably beaten-up looking, suggesting the certainty of hidden treasures. It's not overly gentrified, but some shops are perfectly chic. We used to make an annual pilgrimage there to search for holiday arbors. On one of the first hunting expeditions, we walked into a shop called Gypsy. It was cramped perfectly, and immediately intriguing. But the proprietress was involved in a long conversation and evidently had no intention of ending it. After 10 more minutes of no word from her, we started to walk out. She abruptly stopped the tete-a-tete and asked, 'Can I help you?' I said, yes, do you by chance have any Christmas tree pins? The old lady fixed me with such a suspicious glare, I expected red laser beams to shoot out of her eyes and pulverize me. She kept staring until I asked if there was a problem. She said, in an almost Robert DeNiro tone, 'I'll show you Christmas tree pins,' and started pulling out tray after tray of them from below the counter. Were we in The Twilight Zone? I couldn't believe my eyes, and she couldn't believe I didn't know she was a well-known collector of Christmas tree brooches. I finally convinced her I had no idea, had never heard of her, no one had mentioned a word about her. Estelle wasn't about to part with a single one of them, no matter how much I oohed and ahhed and offered cold hard cash. She lived above the shop and kept her prized, precious collection there. It was enough just to see the pins and hear their stories (and eventually, we even traded a few). The one I coveted most was an unusual blue-glass vintage tree in a golden frame. Behind the glass were what looked like metal jewel cups. I've looked at that tree 100 times (I found one many years later in an antiques mall, prompting extreme hyperventilation) and still can't quite discern what's in there. I still think of it as my gaudy glass Gypsy tree, and never gaze upon it without thinking of Estelle. We went to visit one year, and her shop was closed. Another shop owner told me she'd died. Eventually I tracked down one of her daughters, who said they were going to keep up their mother's collection.

Isn't this tree unique? This is when the lack of a mark is most missed. Who made this crazy Christmas piece? It's vintage, 2-3/4" tall, and rare enough to warrant a $250 price tag.

How Cute Is That?

Christmas, like Easter, is a holiday that allows sophisticates to grow corny and cute. Almost any theme incorporated into a Christmas tree pin seems adorable, just as people not normally into fluffy bunnies and baby chicks get soft on them come March or April.

Christmas tree pins have been shown being decorated by every creature on earth and beyond, from angels to Mickey Mouse. Here, baby bears in Santa caps and bow trim their tree, one standing on a drum to reach the higher branches. Little sister bear, dressed in pink, holds a candy cane and star. The tree itself is highly detailed; $10-20

Animals find themselves frequently affiliated with Christmas tree pin designs. One tree was even planted right on Noah's Ark, amidst all the voyaging pairs. Here, a disparate menagerie groups around a fir: giraffe, panda, penguin, puffin and elephant; $10-20

The tree on right first showed up with a single Leprechaun handling the decorating duties alone on the top of the ladder. Then, the pin became a chatelaine with a very verklempt looking buddy. Who knows what it means, but it's amusing. $10-25

No, the choir of snowboys below is not a tree but, newly found, I had to add it. Their Kringley outfits are festive red felt, their songbooks are marked 'Noel,' and with a flip of a switch the pin plays a Christmas medley. $10-25

The Greatest Gifts

No idea if I love these trees because they were gifts from friends or they really are as clever as I imagine. Most trees girlfriends gave me as gifts turned out to be signed, so these were the only ones I could include in this volume.

Susan's sweet candy Gumdrops Tree pin not only has a red-licorice trunk, it has matching earrings. I love this confection of confetti-glittered plastic and had never seen it before. (Another favorite tree is a striped-cane tree imitating candy, but I couldn't show it here because signed.) The value on the novel Gumdrops tree? You got it: priceless.

Isn't Karen's tree on top wonderful? Children in gaily-colored old-fashioned costumes play Ring Around the Rosey surrounding a decorated Christmas tree. It's a charming and unusual brooch that needs no name or glamorous stones to make it special. Again, priceless because from a friend.

Mary's Snowflakes pin on the right is ingenious in its simplicity, a tree of oversized brass crystals with icy rhinestone jewels, dangling a smaller flake. It was love at first sight for me on this one and it makes an interesting point about where things are. I think Mary said she bought it at Macy's, but this pin did not show up at any of the May department stores I visited that season, so it just goes to show merchandise must be geographically targeted even within large chains.

La-La thought this was the ugliest Christmas tree pin she'd ever seen, and while the sentiment might be Scroogey, I loved it, the Bah Humbug done up so prettily in rich green, dangling with bells and topped with a purple star. (I'm also partial to trees formed by letters or words.)

Finally, Debbie actually *made* the glittery, abstract tree bottom right. Now that's friendship.

Pearls of Not-So-Great Price

Surely among the prettiest Christmas pines are pins decorated with faux pearl ornaments (and more rarely, real pearls). Yet this isn't a highly collected category for some reason, despite the lustrous effect and white pearlescence akin to snow. But gather them together and the trees with pearly snowballs decorating branches make an irresistible aesthetic statement.

The tiny one (on top) originally was made by Marvella, date unknown. Numerous unsigned copies followed. I purchased this one at a Joan Bari shop in 1993 (along with an enormous Ultra-Craft tree that could not have been more its polar opposite); $25. Sticking with trees originally signed, the lettuce-like tree with pearl zigzag (to the right below the Marvella) is originally a Richelieu; unsigned copies ran rampant on the Internet in 1996-97; $25. Next to it, the skinny odd-bodkins tree has been done three ways, in plain gold and also heavily encrusted with bright red and green rhinestones; $25.

The vintage tree (far right) of big pearly orbs probably is not an Xmas botanical, but no one cares, it's so voluptuous, and not particularly easy to find; $50-100. Above it on right (in top row) stands a Pellicious unsigned pine of multicolor gems and pleasing pearl accents; $50+. Back in the second row (on far left), look to what great effect the pearls are shown against deep, bright green, not to mention the fact its golden settings are fully realized ornaments. Clever! $25-50.

The third row includes (left to right) an elegantly enameled holly-leaves vintage tree with both pearls and jewel-tone stones, $50+; a well-cut tannenbaum that for some reason exudes confidence due to ziggy scallops and bulging pearls amid vibrant multicolor crystals also protruding from perches, $25-50; a tailored, patterned stamping with single pearl set into French prongs, $25; and finally in that row, a lovely Lisner retread (what Lisner hasn't been?) of swirling metal ropes, like pearled lassos, studded with icy polychrome teardrops; $25-50.

The trees at ends of bottom row have free-swinging pearl ornaments on soldered rhinestone chain that has grayed gorgeously. In fact, the beauty of these particular oldies comes from the darkening of once brilliant crystals. While unsigned, these creations were also made and signed by Hobe, who may have made one for Hattie Carnegie as well; $75-150 unsigned. Between them sits a vintage version of an unsigned Warner tree usually filled with signature jewel-tone brilliants. Isn't it peachy done in pearls? $50-100.

The Art of Enameling

Not all collectors go ga-ga over glitz. Instead they often find enamels a bigger thrill. In Christmas tree pins, the names Robert, Sandor and Art rule the realm of enameled arbors for their glossy luster, rich depth or frosty finish. Applying vitreous enamel to metal to create vibrant, jewel-like masterpieces is an ancient technique involving fusing powdered glass to a base by firing. The powder melts, flows and hardens to a smooth, durable coating. Whether transparent, opaque or opalescent when fired, different colors are obtained from various metallic oxides. Green and brown, for example, come from iron. The best results require care and multiple firings. Applied enamel paints, of course, don't measure up to fired enamels.

Here are two no-name vintage Christmas tree pins that have nonetheless been lavished with attention when it came to greening their branches. The delicacy of the enameling on the well-cast tree (left) is even lovelier due to cast-metal fringe edging its five tiers. Vitreous brown enamel on trunk is especially glossy. The multicolor crystals are a nice touch for sparkle, but the silver glitter an odd one, an almost cheap option to get the effect of sleet; $50+ Highly detailed holly leaves are a sharp, savage note in antiqued gold metal, all softened with opaque green enameling. The uneven scattering of tiny colored gems like jewel berries, and the clever application of enameled leaves to the pot, are finishing touches that make this vintage tree so special; $50+

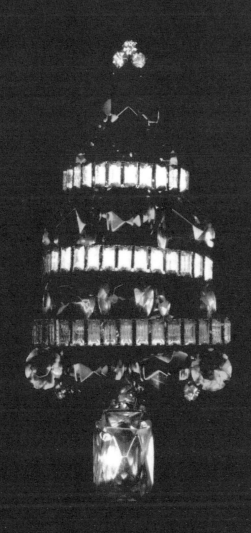

Mystery in Shades of Blue

Genuinely vintage elements always throw a student of jewelry off when assessing age. In this bounteous brooch's case, the fixed, convex, circular rhinestone chain of graying crystal baguettes that serves as 3-D garland is old. The large, splashy blue stones don't look especially new either. The collection of icy blue glass gems, giving the tree a just-fished-from-the-ocean look, consists of faceted teal hearts, pale sapphire teardrops and roses montées, powder-blue brilliants – plus crystal chatons and an oversized emerald-cut stone for the sizable trunk. All are prong-set into a gunmetal setting, lending more antique effect. The long pin stem has its clasp on the lower end, too. It's a commendable effort toward a vintage look, but no one made Christmas trees this size 'way back when,' just shy of 4 inches. It reminds me of a tree available during the 2007 holiday season from Siena Julia, but gone now so impossible to compare exactly. The casting is complicated and may involve much soldering, but so well concealed by the hematite plating it's hard to estimate. Large teardrops are all unfoiled and open in back, so they look extremely liquidy. Teal hearts are pronged into closed settings, so their glistening reflection is deeper. The stones are turned in different directions, and as always, an upside-down heart makes the perfect tree topper because of the point – but even it is decorated with a diamante crown. Will the designer who made this please stand up? $150.

Metallica

Christmas tree pins that carry collectors most quickly back to childhood are brooches that feature metallic Shiny Brite finishes, reminiscent of mercury glass or just the simple red and green orbs that first enchanted us as tots, our earliest memories of holiday tree trimmings. Remember opening up a fresh box, like glass bubbles, from Woolworth's?

Christmas tree pins with metallic ornaments stand out, whether vintage or new. The 1972 classic Eisenberg tree with molded metal balls has been replayed a dozen times by different makers, including the unsigned arbor here (top left), in a pewter finish that makes the metallics pop. It's more engaging than the rhinestone versions any time; $25. Next to it (center top) is one of the first Xmas pins I ever bought, sold in department stores around 1993. Consisting of soldered rhinestone chain and loose rhinestone-chain garland, it's the red and green metallic balls that elevate it up from just another so-so sparkler; $25-50. Metallic paints also color the ornaments on the two trees below it (to the right and left). One uses an old Hollycraft design that typically features faux pearls or RS with aurora borealis film, so the metallics are a breath of fresh air; $25-50. Same with the little Marvella tree (here, unsigned), almost always done in pearls ... so the bright metallic ornaments color it up and add spice; $25. Between them is a tree done in metallic stars, a design usually issued by Kirk's Folly, but here unsigned, and beauty marked with RS inside the golden stars; $25.

The solid-green metallics that give the trees on top right plus middle right and left that cold edge make these pines more interesting than they'd be without a reflective surface. Note the difference between the chillier shiny surface and the warmer, satiny one. The wormy roadmap tree on the right, with glitter and rhinestones, sometimes turns up as a signed Eisenberg. $25 each.

Twin red and green trees in satin metallic are two of my all-time favorites. Why, I can't say. One first appeared at Marshall's back when that chain was a treasure trove of trees (where I also once found the most unlikely Erwin Pearl tree). I love the time that went into conceiving these two brilliantly-tinted tannenbaum: a metal overlay, with cut-out collage of angel, candy cane, holly and boot, is the roof over a mirrored base spacious enough to let you apply lipstick if you want to. The metal layers are swedged together. And check out those circusy trunks. Crazy. Companies that put thought and effort into their holiday pieces rock. If these remain uncommon, $50-100+. I just can't tell yet how many were out there.

At base stands an enormous brooch valued as a keepsake souvenir of one of the first articles I wrote about Christmas tree pins in 2000, in either Mary Engelbreit's *Home Companion* ... or was it *Collectibles* magazine? It had this as the title. What a massive brooch it is, three metallic pines on a snow-traced ground that's almost 4 inches wide and over 2-1/2 inches tall. The company that made this had to be cuckoo for Christmas. Not too many of these around, do you think? $50-100.

Tope Chest

The Greek term for ornamental gardening involves training, cutting and trimming trees or shrubs into odd or ornamental shapes. How lovely we know when the very first Christmas topiary tree pin was made. Cartier Paris did the honors with an Art Deco *chef d'oeuvre* in the Twenties.

Two costume versions of the original antique Cartier have been created. Here is the vintage version of it, top left. Soldered, plated rhinestone chain forms the topiary shape, while red brilliants and green ovals are prong-set into the pave-effect background. In the Cartier original, white gold, diamonds, rubies and emeralds serve as the precious glitter, so no wonder it has sold at auction for as high as $50,000. That makes this seem like a bargain at $150+

Next to the faux French is a perky topiary with red bow dressing up deep green ground studded with crystal-clear rhinestones. It looks like a Lianna piece, with the tapestry pattern overlaid with translucent epoxy. 1990s, $50+. Above it to right is a favorite find, charming down to the last detail, also possibly a Lia creation. A big ball of red poinsettias centered with topaz rhinestones is offset with blue-black berry beads wired on to the bounteous bouquet. A swirled pole is beribboned with a bow and all is packed into one of the all-time great pots, red and white with holly-leaf motifs and paint splashes mimicking teeny berries. $50+

The oddball limestone confection on left has a sort of atomic look with mushroom flower. Refreshing to find this shade of citrus, you'll also turn it up occasionally in different colorations, including a pattern with red and dark green. It's a great vintage design, $50+

Why are two Aquarium Christmas trees on this page? No idea. But here they are, looking like kelp and seaweed caught under glass for the holidays. Each one is slightly different. These are 21st Century brooches sold through a national catalogue and proved popular with collectors; $50-75.

Intriguing Trees

Some pins you could stare at all season long. You know them. You have some. They possess an ingenious little facet, a twist, an element out of the norm. Here are some that have It.

The Atomic Flora tree appears a second time in this book, dressed in different colors. It's clever in any color, sort of futuristic and feminine at once. The atomic effect is carried out in the trunk. This one's a stumper in terms of age; it's not new, but probably looks older than it actually is; $50+

The angel-topped teardrops tree is from 1993, purchased in a department store during the last gasp of the great old jewelry names (before manufacture went overseas). I'm 90% certain it came from the Trifari section counter. Monet is another possibility, but I'm more confident it was Trifari. Names meant nothing to me back then, so I let it slip from memory; $75-150. Something about the polished, dainty emerald-navettes tree next to it echoes the other's sensibility, and they appear to have been made by the same company or designer; $25-50.

Second row: Shooting stars encase what looks like a large chunk of emerald glass that's more likely Lucite. It's a special tree that is relatively scarce and has all the bells and whistles, from ingenious design to attention to trunk detail. Trees with glass or Lucite encased by a decorative metal frame are just unbeatable. (The star is identical to the one in top row right and considering the rest of its attributes as well, may have been made by the same company.) $150. The middle tree has all the earmarks of an Original by Robert and well may be. (There simply is no place for the signature palette cartouche.) The trunk is identical to signed Roberts, as is the twisted trunk and the particular star. The tree's body consists of big, juicy cabochon navettes in emerald, hung with faceted ruby beads and rhinestone chain garland; $75-150. On the right is another of those trees within a tree that's so terrific, the interior textured gold set with flower-effect rhinestones thanks to the decorative faux prongs, and the exterior tree is a green-enameled outline. The open space between the two adds dimension. The textured star echoes the inside tree, while the green baguettes in the trunk flash on the exterior arbor. $75-150.

Third row top left: Most collectors would bet this antiqued gold loops tree sports a Hollycraft or Weiss mark. It's a primitive or barbaric beauty with deep-gold finish, its navette stones darkened, the whole piece rich with a vintage patina. But it's unsigned; $50-100. An unusual, heavy, cast, filigree-effect vintage tree of dark gold metal that makes the polychrome aurora borealis stones pop and glitter. The cabbage-like clusters are appealing and neither the star nor trunk are status quo, so it's especially eye-catching; $75-100. If simplicity itself is a turn-on, the open-work vintage tree with stark, baguette candles is a thrill. The scores and notches make the ropy metal look needled, and the whole thing just works, from the many colors of the candlesticks to the truly unique truck; $75-150. It's surprising how closely related the fancy frills tree far right is to the plain Jane next to it. The reverse sides are extremely similar, as if the jewelry company wanted one bare bones model and the other dressed to the nines. The larger stones in a rainbow of colors look brilliant against all the smaller emerald crystals, and the milky candle baguettes are starkly stunning; $75-150.

Shell 'n Tell

Creative souls took the time and care to color and layer shell pieces onto clear celluloid backings for out-of-the-ordinary holiday pins. Clockwise from top left: a small shell tree pin of forest green, heavily showered with multicolor rhinestones, $10; layered veggie-green shell wreath studded with ruby-red rhinestones like holly berries, $10-25; bounteously layered iridescent pink shelled Christmas tree pin with star, real-look brown trunk, and variety of glittering rhinestone ornaments; $50. The tall shell pin on left is what it is, a whole shell with multicolor faux pearls, $50. S'wonderful.

Geometree

Three related geometric Christmas tree pins (top row) from the 1990s. Look how little the two green pines differ from each other. One is all enamel-epoxy, the other features rhinestones. Did one wholesaler, manufacturer or jewelry house create two slightly different versions for two different retailers? The tree at center between them is a twin to the more terrific unsigned tree on p. 106 of Mary Morrison's first edition. This one is an openwork tree, while Mary's featured epoxied panels. Greens, $10-20; openwork, $25-50.

Multiplication Tale

Collectors can find twin and triplet groupings of Christmas trees galore. These three are all from the 21st Century: On top, rhinestone-chain in Christmas-color crystals, soldered together, makes a festive sparkler that wouldn't makes waves even at the office; $10-$25. The pair o' pines is cute for its multi-patterned boughs, from green dotted tiers to red cross hatches, blue checkerboard and yellow grain; $10-25. The tree-o at right is aesthetically pleasing with varying sizes and two elements of greenery flanking a silver tree with red tinsel; $10-25.

Seeing Red

Even more than green, red is the primary color of Christmas. We've almost always had a red living room (still do), so it's pretty much toujours the holiday season at our house whether intended or not. Because red is so fiery and intense (and as a wearable color loaded with negatives because of its historical connotations), how nice red at least gets its glory every December.

An attention-getting story went out on the newswires a few years ago, worth mentioning in case you missed it. An avid Christmas tree pin collector died and directed that her wake at the funeral home be done to the nines in Christmas decorations, with carols playing, trees trimmed with lights and ornaments. Her daughters presented mourners each with a Christmas tree pin as a keepsake of their mother. Undoubtedly it was the most memorable send-off visitors had ever experienced.

The mostly red trees shown here are loud and merry. The tree like a spade (on top) has an icy faceted trillian-cut glass stone wedged into a faux marcasite metal frame. Though smallish, it packs a punch because of the rich cherry hue and muted metal making primary red pop even more. It's a tree of the Nineties, issued by Latasia and also boxed in department stores under the Investments name; $25-50

The two trees in the second row showcase a riot of rhinestones and are special because vintage, not simply two more brand new pines, part of the current avalanche. The quantity of new rhinestone trees being made and flooding the market is so vast, it snows you under. An unquenchable passion for glitz or desire to own every tree made is the only reason any collector would consider snapping up the full reach of razzmatazz. But the pre-glut oldies are special, tokens of a time holiday trees were just glittering wearables. The fancy brooch on left has icy jeweled swags accenting ruby brilliants, reds that enjoy a second jolt of color courtesy of orangey teardrops. As accents, red rhinestones (right) make this abstract tree what it is; $50-150 each.

The large Christmas tree (center) looks vintage thanks to the dark, hematite finish but is new, a large trellis overgrowing with jewel flora, the depth and color of which remove it from the realm of the ordinary. It's a fantastic tree, with a value lowered only because of its profusion, still being sold on the market; $25-50.

The spiraled emeralds winding around the vintage tree bottom left are heightened because of the bright metallic red paint, especially frisky and festive here; $50+

The circles of light trees comprise clever designs, one a vintage tree (lower right), one contemporary (bottom), which harkens back to the oldie. Three soldered circlets of rhinestone chain define the old tree and have pastel navettes dangling centrally – an odd color choice since the trunk shows off jewel-tone ruby navettes in sideways and vertical settings; $50-150. The new tree is brilliantly conceived, rhinestone chain and rounds draped precisely to suggest a tree, boughs and shape formed by the number of circles, each like a wreath hosting red or green teardrop stone. $25-50

Jinglers, Janglers, Tremblers, Danglers

Extras in the form of gifts, poinsettias, boots, candy canes, Teddy bears, bells, sleds and ornaments lend Christmas trees heightened interest, especially when they jingle and move. In the first two trees shown (opposite page), the wired-on additions of gaily wrapped gifts, red flora and green holly leaves literally make these trees, turning unremarkable tannenbaum into serious charmers. It would be better if they trembled, but the extras are wired on and fixed, unfortunately; $25-50 each.

The big pine laden with charms is a Holidays 1998 brooch from a Dallas boutique, and was expensive. The large golden charms jangle nicely when worn and contrast fashionably with the red and green above; $75-100.

The next three on the left side are all simply colorful and cheerful, with not much to add except they are pleasing; $10-25. The silvery, starred sapling, however, with enameled charms dangling from all over the boughs, was sold in a shop at the Zoppini modular charms counter, so it may be from Zoppini, but no one could answer that query at the time; $25-50.

On its right is a vintage modified-circle pin encompassing a Christmas tree, those cocktail-tomato cabs representing holly berries, and dangling, swinging ornaments; $25+

The open-loop confection of brilliant red and green boughs (bottom left) is an early 1990s pin, one of the first 'new' trees purchased, and has an especially nice array of enameled charms that make the tree more special; $25-50. The Santa tree is much newer (2000s), but also has a punchy panoply of chained-on charms, adding length and interest to an already eye-catching portrait tree; $25-50.

The tree of golden stars centered by crystal rhinestones is much more worthy of a look due to its colorful arrangement of packages, $25. Below it (left) is an oddball design in terms of tree shape, the banner-like wreath around it evidently dictating the reverse stagger; $25+.

Far right, that pine with needled boughs is a classic, especially with bright-red dangling bells that shimmy when you wear it and move; $25-50, depending on whether vintage or newer.

Rue de Rivolis

The fancy-cut stones called rivolis, whether scalloped, cupcake, torpedo, margaritas (marguerites), are favorites of jewelry collectors and cause a stir in Christmas tree pins even though the results aren't always exactly elegant. In fact, if some of the vintage trees did enjoy a much greater design aesthetic, it would be easier to insist they might have come out of Miriam Haskell's house, since some of the construction is right: perforated metal, wired stones, metal backings covering the wire work and unsightly perfs. The earliest Christmas tree pin known unequivocally as Haskell's dates to 1993, but speculation on these older specimens is still good sport because they really are Miriamesque.

All that's known for sure about old Christmas tree brooches loaded with radiant rivolis and marguerites is that Weiss did attach its name to some of them, so the question is, how many of these are unsigned Weiss? One Weiss knockoff uses all heliotrope margaritas, but the signed Weiss trees usually go with vitrail medium rivolis.

Never pass one up, signed or not. If you don't want it, someone will. The trees here include vintage twins (top) with loopy filigree boughs set with purple-green watermelon tourmaline (vitrail medium) margs and purple cabochons, the other with flowery jonquil color in stones, each tree with palm-tree fronds above trunks; $75-125.

Down and to the right is a clunky rope-tiered tannenbaum with deep emerald fluted rivolis tipped with metal studs and green-brilliant accents, $50-100. Below that one is a more petite pine that sloppily shows those perforations, $25-50. Veer directly to the far left of that small tree and find a pin with forest-green torpedo rivolis, also tipped with metal, $50-100. To its right is another tree of iridescent jonquil marguerites, $75-100.

The tree at center is perhaps most Haskellesque, faceted Lucite beads with seed-bead tips, the 20 green-hinted crystal beads holiday icy, all wired on to a perforated metal backing covered with a solid metal base; $75-150. To its left is a vintage sparkler of rhinestone disco balls each finished with a prong-set chaton, another that has Haskell attributes; $75-150.

The five-piece forest row on the low level obviously doesn't belong on the rue de rivoli but arrived here and just didn't get kicked out. Any of the first four could be vintage Hobe trees, with that tell-tale curlicue filigree, $25-50 each. On the far right, a tree of unfinished metal hosting ruby and emerald stones, relates to the tree far left, but is sans curlicue; $10-25.

Pine Pin Potpourri I

The wildly disparate Christmas tree pins here have little in common but their pindom. Left to right from top:

Off-kilter 2007 tree (inadvertently left off the 2007-earmarked page), its tilted and the oddly-shaped star giving it an even dizzier imbalance. What's not to love? $25. Vintage maze tree with a smattering of jewels in a row, could be a birthstone tree for someone with the right birth months in the fam; $50. Cute 2006 Walgreen's trembler tree with cheerful painting and brightly colored jingle bells set *en tremblant* on springs, $25+. Well-conceived circles tree, highly appealing, mid-90s from Marshall's, brilliant use of scattered stones within select open circles, $50. Look what boughs of molded balls and staggered levels can offer when mixed with Christmas-colored stones; $25+. Right, vintage stepped-edge openwork tree with metallic red ornaments and draped green tinsel, $25-50.

Witty wire tree looks like it's composed of golden paperclips. This one has a fancy base that allows it to stand up, and emerald and ruby stones prong-set along the vertical strands, $75-100. Simple vintage tree that looks like a large star trailing comets that finish in a flash of sparkle, $50. Enamel-drenched pine in green and cream boughs, sometimes signed Hedy, this one not, $25-50. Tiny tree pin with metallic green ornaments and a red bottom border, $10-20. Huge plastic vintage tree with silver-metallic finish, the shine setting off the colorful ornaments, star and candy cane, $50. Mint-green vintage tree with hints of snow on tips of tiers, a sprightly star and rainbow of rhinestones making it even merrier; $50.

Featherweight filigree tree probably made in Mexico, $25-50. Old-fashioned alphabet tree of silver, almost gothic in its print font, $75-125. Another wirework tree that looks like paperclips, again studded with well-placed jewels, $50+. Metallic-green and silver-plated lightning tree, effective even if inexpensive, $10-25.

Plastic plaid 'Merry Christmas' tree of acrylic (missing its star), $25-50. Next to it, a maroon-trimmed tree we can consider with all the maroon trees below it, all possibly from the same company, successfully using the same hues of hushed gold, wine and green. One duplicates the wonderful Jonette jester tree. All of them, because of the maroon coloration, are eye-catching and fetching; $25-50 each. Moving back up to the first maroon row, a tiny little vintage tree is beautifully cast and hung with jadeite beads plus faulx pearls, $25+. The feathery openwork tree is a *trompe l'oeil* fooler, with its 'stones' actually globs of epoxy, $10-25. Below it is a triple-threat trio of trees with scalloped boughs and oversized stars, $25. The simple, flat golden vintage tree on right is greatly enhanced by an array of colorful cabochons, $25-50.

The solid-maroon tree (bottom, toward right) resembles David Wright sheet-metal pins, but is instead a humble metal shape with enamel paint, $25+. Finally, still another tree starring gingerbread men among cocktail-tomato balls, $25+.

True Colors

A 3-D tree chock full o' crystals, harboring pewter presents below, $25+. Two copies of the busy but elegant and rare Regency tree, $25 each. Bodice brooch features bows stretched between RS circle buttons, flat back, purchased in Florida around 2000; $25-50. Tree far right looks like a mini-version of the large Butler-Wilson tree, ripe with faceted stones, $25-50.

Closely set emerald RS give an open-work pine oomph, as do the rubies in pot and the diamond dangles, $25. Fabulous filigree fir, the gold pattern punctuated with red RS and outline in emerald RS chain, $50+. The all-gold tree and his sister to the right are fraternal twins, one lavished with flat-back Swarovski stones, the result a rich, heavily encrusted, gemmy beauty; $25+ and $50+. A Hobé-like tree, its interior filled with golden leaves, RS berries and thin curlicues, $50.

Elaborate red, clear and green tree of dainty RS chain, the lower tier articulated and swingy. This is a new copy of a vintage Hattie Carnegie tree, probably made in China, $25+. Flat, coated-plastic Taiwan tree notable for its unusual colors, harlequin diamond pattern and red bows, $25. Crocodile Christmas tree (who cares if it's a gator?) features Santa-capped swamp creature rowing his tree back home to the bayou, $25-50. Cheap, painted, plastic tree with gifts, slightly captivating because of its colors, $25-50.

School-theme tree with all the familiar props, apple and bell to ABCs and blackboard, colorfully enameled and raised against a flat background of lacquered glitter, $25-50. Another childhood tree, this one icy silver draped with thick red ribbon and a cast of characters including snowman, angels and gingerbread boy, $25. Finally, a triptych of snow people, $25-50, two from the 21st Century and the third a vintage snowman with top hat and snow-laden tree. Most collectors prefer vintage to new, but those sparkling stones mixed with enamels, and the second one all tangled with lights, are hard to resist if you collect guys with trees.

Election 2008!
Hillary & Elephant

56

The Glitter Factor

Increasing numbers of collectors are decorating their Christmas trees with Christmas tree pins. Some are amazing arrangements, and the trees on the opposite page are perfect for such sparkling endeavors because they pick up the glow of the tiny tree lights so beautifully.

You can of course wear and collect these as you would any others, but the glitter factor is a bonus for decoration. Some collectors are nutty for these ostentatious rhinestone concoctions, almost all new, many made to order for dealers who saw they could make money by selling them. They assumed the glitzier species would sell best.

The teardrops-lasso tree on top left may also be found as an older piece signed Lisner or MJEnt. This is a new copy and is pleasing in every way; $25+. Continuing across the top row stand two new trees that are all rhinestone, the first plain merry with its colors, the second one in the style of Hobe; $15-25.

The next group features a wonderful invention in the category, trees that contain a figural motif within the arbor. Candles, crosses, Santa, snowmen or wreaths are enclosed within the tree borders for a clever twist. Skipping across the row: an openwork emerald, peridot and fuchsia tree holding a RS candle, finished with a gold-plated bow and pinwheel star, $25; big rock candy Christmas tree also holding a candle inside, this one alternating frosted givre baguettes and fat roses montees, with mixed-green navettes, oversized star and upside-down emerald cabochon teardrop trunk (not to mention the sapphire-baguette candle with orange RS flame), $25+; barbaric brooch on right encloses a top-hatted snowman and has those great, sharp, skinny green navettes set so their points jut out for a wild, jungle effect, $25-50; back toward the left see an icy, openwork tree showing a cross, its rhinestone chain with baguette accents all aurora borealis causing that iridescent blue cast, $25-50; the fat baguette givre stones in the white and peridot tree surround a hard-to-discern candle inside, tiny RS chain lending cold grit to the smoother, frosted-glass baguettes that look like geometric icicles, $25-50; and the crystal tree on right boasts an easy-to-spot holiday wreath plus a second figural, an angel in place of the usual star; $25-50.

Bottom row: The flattest tree ever made is intriguing due to the color variations on the soldered RS chain, creating a pattern of ruby, emerald, peridot and diamond all mixed in, punctuated with a sparkling 'diamond' base, $25-50. The second tree is slightly older, a crafts or homemade project using celadon and topaz stones on a perforated-metal base, $25+ The arrow or chevron tree is eye-catching due to well-placed, contrasting stones against the crystal diamante chain, rich, jewel-tone accents of marquis and round faux emeralds, $50. Sinuous center line runs up the midline of this tree like a silvery snake midst vibrant jewels in many shapes and sizes, $25-50.

Instant Messaging

The rarest unsigned Christmas tree pin with a message is a big hunk of vintage metal that mechanically pulls apart vertically to reveal a cheerful red 'Merry Christmas.' It is heavy and well-made. A friend actually owns this scarce specimen but was in the midst of an interstate move when trees were being photographed and had no idea where it was at that time. For a company to put that much effort and elaborate detail into a holiday piece creates a special circumstance, so in terms of collectibility, it is high on the totem pole, with a value likely in the $300-500 range.

Back down on earth, trees that speak to us create a jolly category, one a collector could go after exclusively. They range from vintage to new. In signed pins, Lianna probably has the most messages to its credit. In unsigned, who knows?

The oldest trees with wordplay shown on the opposite page are the two fir-swagged pines heralding 'Jesus' and 'X-Mas.' Neither vintage tree is particularly easy to find, so they rate a $50 value for what they have to say.

The golden stack of letters that spells out 'Merry Christmas' is likely a Nineties 'homage' to Robert Lee Morris' 1993 kindred tree of gold, hard to find and expensive. This uncommon, well-made costume-jewelry knockoff gains value due to its relationship with a rare tree. So, while plain, it may be valued at $50-100.

The two most novel arbors are the sign-language pine that handily spells out 'I Love You,' and a two-part pin of stamped tree attached to festive signage, directing onlookers to 'Kiss Me! It's Christmas!' $25-50. Who needs mistletoe?

The polymer clay cane tree is colorful and quirky with its kooky, oversized wire star; $25-50. The star-topped 'Joy to the World' tree next to it was part of a series with different pronouncements; $25. An enameled Christmas tree accents the vintage pin wishing all a 'Merry Christmas,' $25.

At either end of the second row, both the biased-set 'Merry Christmas' pine with green enamel and red rhinestones and the 'kisses and hugs tree decorated with Xs and Os look like Lianna creations but are unmarked; $25-50 each. An angel accent adds interest to the vintage 'Joy' pin, just as bright holly does for the nicely made 'Seasons Greetings' tree; $25 each. The little vintage 'Jesus' tree on bottom appeals to Christians determined to proclaim belief in the real reason for the season – right on the lapel; $10.

Kiss Me
It's Christmas!

Christmas

Joy
To the
WORLD

Merry
Christmas

XOXO
XOXO
XOXO
XOXO

JOY

MERRY
CHRISTMAS

MERRY
CHRISTMAS

SEASONS
GREETINGS

Jesus

JESUS

XMas

... It's Time for Mistletoe & Holly

The deep green of holly leaves and their red-berry fruit are natural components of fantasy Christmas tree pins. The rarest vintage holly-berry tree in the signed universe is probably by Freirich; the rarest (signed PV) mistletoe tree is the elegant brooch that's the star of the plot line in *Cult of the Christmas Tree Pin*, also on the cover of that mystery novel. Beyond the signed beauties, most holly trees are anonymous, although clues suggest some of their provenance.

The trio of holly bouquets next door, the ones tied with ribbon bows (golden or red), have the same unique construction on reverse, an open, ribbed base onto which is swedged the holly-leaves layer. That singular construction is also peculiar to certain known vintage Gem-Craft trees, so one can assume Gem-Craft manufactured and possibly had design input into these beautifully made arbors. The richly enameled red bow on one also suggests Weiss as a possible destination for this design, since a vintage signed-Weiss Christmas tree features this same bow on its branches. These charming bow-tied trees turn up with some regularity, keeping values from being where they should be on such lovely holiday specimens; $25-50.

Consider the uppermost tree, with holly leaves appearing as sharp as in real life thanks to the jagged gold edging; the red berries are beads that recall the cocktail-tomato ornaments of which Castlecliff was fond. This is an extremely handsome and dimensional vintage holly bush; $25-50

Directly below the top tree is a puzzling one with big, fat berries. The confusion isn't just that the green foliate motif is quite floral, the leaves like petals, but that this tree turns up as surely contemporary and certainly vintage. It's been for sale at retail brand new, but also on its original old vintage card, each tree identical to the other. It's an appealing tree in person, so in fact age becomes less important; $25.

The two trees on either side of the second row are contemporary trees not without their festive charms; $10-25.

Directly below them on each side of the bottom row are two more modern trees, also with something to recommend them. On the left in subtle golden hue is a 3-D creation originally designed long enough ago to make it vintage, but still being designed in the 1990s. Watch for it in an older, enameled version, which as you can imagine is even prettier; $25-50. The hollied tree on right is a bargain at $10, with golden vine tendrils running up through epoxied leaves among multicolor rhinestone berries, all topped with a pave-set star.

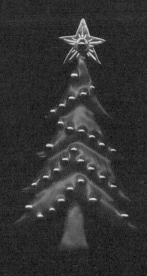

The Presence of Pines Past

One way to separate old from new in trees when you aren't sure is size. (Another way, which a good friend of mine discovered, is that most vintage pins feature their clasps on the bottom rather than top of the pin mechanism.) While suspect sellers suggest all sorts of big Christmas brooches are older, the vast majority aren't. It didn't seem to dawn on many designers of old that something merry might also be mighty (in stature). That said, some larger vintage trees do exist and are fun to find.

The three trees here were my first large-sized discoveries, so the excitement I felt at first sight (so long ago) still lingers. Atop the trio is a gloppy 3-inch enamel Christmas tree brooch, the green boughs and brown trunk thick with dense, opaque color, and surely far removed from refined, but still fetching – perhaps because of the golden, molded-ball trim and the Keith Haring-like etoile with its star-beam engraving that makes it look like it belongs in one of his brilliant grafittis. $25-50

At center is a swedged-construction of tealy-turquoise baked enamel on metal. Hard to tell whether it is a double or triple layer, but appears to be solid base topped by an openwork tree sandwiching a smaller solid tree, all three decks riveted together at star and trunk. The star is part of the openwork layer. This 3-1/4-inch vintage piece is certainly inelegant, but charming in its simplicity and slightly offbeat color. $25-50

On the lower end of the diagonal is a dimensional tree of metallic-satin enameling, its five tiers defined by silver-plated swaths, each decorated with glassy, bezel-set ruby-red cabochon igloos, 11 in all. This 3-1/4-inch convex creation features great attention to detail, from the bark-effect silver trunk to a large, textured star centered with a glittering crystalline rhinestone. An older, smaller, less attractive but exact version of this arbor is featured in *All My Baskets*. $50-100

Festive Framework

Like a tiny shadow box, the first brooch is a gold metal frame with glass top, the interior recessed and backed with red felt. A pictorial collage creates old-fashioned nostalgia inside: bejeweled tree and wreath, cotton-bearded Santa, and a panoply of little brass toys (rodeo rider, ballerina, bonneted ducky) adds interest and dimension to the paper gifts represented beneath them. 2-1/2 inches, $50-100. Next to it is contemporary Christmas eye candy, a brilliant holiday-colors tree inside red rectangle, all the translucent epoxy over patterned metal that shows through; 1-7/8 inches, $25. Top right, a brass base is covered with frosty baked enamel boasting a festive fir with bough-tip red candles; 2 inches, $25. On the left, a disc of bisque is kiln-fired to produce glossy graphics of two pines in snow under a starry midnight sky; 1-3/8 inches, $10.

In the bottom row, beads define the pine created within a golden metal frame, all reminiscent of an abacus. Clever concept, with wires stretching side to side and loose beads lined up along the horizontal wirework. Gold beads mark the exterior tree shape against blue background beading, contrasting pine green within the tree. A single red bead tops the tree. 1-5/8-inches square, $25. Finally, an Alpine scene is rendered on deep cobalt blue painted with gold leaf on a fired bisque. 2-1/8 inches, $25.

Pine Pin Potpourri II

Presenting a melange of mixed greens with nary a single thing in common but unique design. Left to right:

1. Heavy vintage tree of etoiles with sunny yellow-gold startop, $50.
2. Sweet lime-sherbet tree with preppie pink RS, from Michael's, $10-25.
3. Vintage copy of a Mylu tree, golden filigree trellis overlay with RS, riveted to pleasing green-washed base with thoughtfully designed star and trunk, $50.
4. Vintage Happy Face tree that belongs in every collection's pop-culture category, deep, dark colors that make the yellow icon pop, $50+. Its twin, one jump over ...
5. Vintage yellow star tree just like the Happy Face tree but done with bright jaune five-pointer, $10-25.
6. Snowman tree, highly coveted Christmas brooch of red neige-niks, their little golden top hats and stick arms defining them but still hard for many to discern, $50+
7. Scarlet-bow'd Parfait tree, layered pave boughs and green epoxy, sweet, $10-25.
8. Robin Hood tree features lace-up green satin ribbon running through perforated holes in silver metal, $25-50.
9. Bunch o' Pine Boughs tree, colorful rhinestone'd version and unsigned copy of both the Jay Strongwater for Nordstrom brooch and the 2004 Avon tree; this one, $10-25.
10. Back to the left, a strangely concave vintage tree of curvilinear forest-green triangle resembling the work of Beatrix, but unsigned, $25+
11, 12. Extra Tall Skinny Xmas trees, both vintage, notable for their long, slender shapes. The one on the right was an early favorite, metallic green mixing with gold balconies on the tower. $25-50 each.
13. Technicolor Tannenbaum, one of the great castings, surely Beatrix but unsigned, a vintage desirable that has it all: vivid metallics, jeweled multicolor bells, needled swags, candles and a ribbon banner running casually through the boughs. Fabulous, $100-150.
14. Polychrome Splash tree, another early favorite with the most unusual construction: thin, flexible metal is bent into a zig-zag form, the silver base painted with red and green epoxy, edged or centered with crystal studs. Large and unique, $50+
15. Vintage circles tree with another of the bright-yellow enamel stars, $10-25.
16, 17. Sack o' Tree pins, two bags of pine (or is the first one an ornament rather than bag?), one in metal with enamel and RS, the other a resin with childlike primary colors; $10-50 each, depending on availability versus scarcity.
18. Three-candle tree, one of my first vintage veterans and so, beloved; flat green with silver candles, simplicity itself; $25.
19. Fourteen-candle tree, one of the great beauties, sometimes signed MJ Ent, here not. What excellent casting to produce the detailed golden needles, all accented with icy candlesticks. Dimensional, layered and swedged, this is a great beauty; $50-100
20. Trembler tree, an openwork goldie with 10 red epoxy bows set en tremblant on every tier, including the starbow, $25-50.
21. Plastic, epoxy and beads tree that probably should not be shown in an unsigned-jewelry book because the CKO or KCO letter beads actually stand for a children's charity but which one it was has been forgotten. In person, it's actually real eye candy; $25+
22. Heavily enameled vintage tree that sometimes turns up signed Torino. This unsigned specimen is lovely with the mixed-color stones and candle baguettes gone milky; $25+.
23. The 3-D Golden Girl is a vintage pin that, when trimmed with rhinestone-chain garland, sometimes turns up signed Hattie Carnegie. This bare-branched unsigned version is as sharp and incredibly dimensional as the Hattie, and with a smattering, scattering of small, clear baguettes insinuating candles; $50+
24. Silvery Scotch pine is a smaller, less elaborate version of the bounteous golden needles tree above it, pretty nonetheless; $25-50.
25, 26. Two small, simple vintage candled trees, one angular, one needled; $10-25 each.

Antique Plastique

Oh, the joys of historical fact. Invented in 1869 by the Hyatt brothers, celluloid was the first successful thermoset plastic. It could be molded using heat and pressure into fixed shapes (such as Christmas trees). Its use in jewelry enjoyed a heyday from about 1900 to 1930, so when you have a celluloid Xmas brooch, you can be certain you have something old.

While no one froths at the mouth with excitement over celluloid Christmas tree pins, largely because they aren't glamorous, bejeweled or extravagantly carved (as some Bakelite or Lucite pins are), such old-fashioned brooches carry great sentiment: many Baby Boomers remember well their grandmothers pinning the plastic pines on to coat lapels every holiday season.

Celluloid Christmas tree pins may be found in one of four colors: green, creamy white, gilded, pink. Ornamentation includes plastic beads with satinoire faux moonstone effect, or confetti glitter. Considering other old-fashioned antique celluloid items, from fancy buttons to the angel who graces the top of our tree every year, it seems more imagination could have gone into Christmas tree pins for a more captivating result, but they do have their charms. Most trees are thick enough they have not snapped in half due to old plastic gone brittle, but occasionally the thin, molded candles have broken off.

It's good to recall celluloid's original or intended *raison d'etre*: as an albeit unsuccessful substitute for the ivory required to make balls for the wildly popular game of billiards, to stop the slaughter of herds of elephants, massacred for their tusks.

The panoply of celluloid pins on the opposite page range from $10+ for the small size up to $50 for tree and wreath sets.

The bottom row features acrylic plastic trees of recent years. The two on the right light up with the push of a button; $10-29

Rhinestone Refinement

Even non-tree collectors are swept up by the design of some Christmas arbors, and these are two. The delicacy of the first vintage tree comes from its profusion of tiny stones creating the effect of sparkling diamond dust; the thin, patterned silvery metal; and its 'fold-out' convex center panel that sits forward on the brooch. The refinement carries on in all the beautiful details, from the horizontally set baguette finishing the trunk to the delicate, embossed star with a brilliant stone. This vintage tree is similar to an unmarked Hedy tree (identifiable only because it's been found in its original box); $100-150. The elegant Chrysler Building Christmas tree brooch is an Art Deco masterpiece, with downward-curved tiers of stark crystal baguettes, each bough punctuated with brilliants. It is rhodium-plated and 2-1/2 inches tall; $150-250.

This Is Costume Jewelry

You understand the term costume jewelry most clearly when you see color variations that allow a fashionista to choose between gold and silver, green and red, pearls and rhinestones, to suit an outfit best. Of course, when someone likes a tree a lot, period, all colors must be collected. I've long tried to *not* find color variations intriguing, but failed. When the design is desirable, different colors bring a freshness that makes each brooch seem unique. (The pretty fan tree in the chapter on blues was made in five different tones, all crave-worthy. Or take a signed tree such as the Lea Stein Paris: same tree, seven different colors – and collectors wanted all of them.)

The 1990s trees at opposite ends of top row came in green, red and gold. The colors are preferable because they set off the tree's attributes best, from leaf effect to the string of rhinestone lights and belligerent star. The all-gold melts into a subtle blend; $50 each. The three bow-topped trees with streamer garlands delight due to a unique design concept and gritty multicolor stones against the metals. They are 21st-Century pins but look much older, especially the pot metal version; $50 each. Second row: Pearly vintage trees suggest Marvella products, but are unsigned. The glittering rhinestone version is harder to find; $25-50 each. Bottom row: The tree on each end may be found in dozens of permutations and may have been made over several decades, 1970s-90s. Some are better made and cast than others; $25+ each. In the center grows a pair of pines reminiscent of jeweled, enameled or gilded seaweed, airy with openwork metal; $25-50.

Faux La-La-La-La

It's safe to say the majority of signed Christmas tree pins that are either valuable, popular or irresistibly well-designed have been knocked off, usually in China but sometimes in Rhode Island. I've told the story many times about walking innocently into a Manhattan costume jewelry shop in 1998 filled to the gills with glittering eye candy, and the proprietress asked, "Do you like Weiss Christmas tree pins?" Yes, I replied guilelessly, salivating as she reached to open a drawer I expected to reveal a single vintage brooch. Instead, it was full of an army of newly recruited mercenaries, each geometric triangle set off-kilter onto that classic slash trunk and loaded with fluted blue rivolis. The fake Weiss pins and the experience were eye-opening in every way.

The most controversial copy to follow that Weiss was the bare-sticks Hollycraft with dangling bead ornaments. The authentic vintage version is fairly uncommon, but suddenly it was everywhere, coming out of Florida and the Northeast. After that, the dam just broke. Knockoffs grew wild. Dorothy Bauer's bedazzling beauties seemed to crank out of Chinese factories, rendered flat and lifeless, a week after the real thing hit the market.

No name is immune, as we can see on the following page. When even Swarovski copies (unsigned, granted) began showing up, I called the company to ask, what up? A spokeswoman said there was nothing they could do about it.

The top-center tree of silvery see-saws copies a hard-to-find St. John tree. St. John is no longer in the holiday jewelry market, so most of the company's trees are highly desirable, but this is one of the toughest gets when authentic. The copy here is a shadow of the brawnier and more beautiful real thing, but clearly it has a unique design aesthetic. As the copy has gotten more common, its value has dropped to about $25-40. The real St. John tree brooch is $250+ when found.

Flanking the curved-bar Christmas creation are two trees several collectors own as Swan-signed Swarovski saplings, one in silver-plated metal, one in gold plate, the boughs encrusted with pave-set stones and larger peridot-hued navettes and brilliants. These copies are excellently made and beautifully cast; $50 each.

In the center is a heavily jeweled, jazzed-up version of a simple metal Mylu Christmas tree pin. This one is arguably more attractive than the plain-Jane oldie, but the original metal Mylu has its charms, with poly-textured finishes and offbeat modernism. That modern shape comes through even under all the jewels and makes this a primo pine; $50. To its left is a wonderful vintage design yet a poor knockoff of the rare and complicated vintage Har tree; $50+

The trees on lower right and at bottom each are Mylu copies, scrawnier than the always full-bodied Borofsky-Gordon products, but with appeal nevertheless. The lowest tree copies a marvelous Mylu with candy-cane stripes bell-shaped body, its star a riot of holly leaves and berries. This one, different with its metallic green body, has a topper more like a red poinsettia; $50-100. And above it, a poorly designed tree many companies copied, in different colors, gold to green. The signed Mylu version had full branches, more of them, and stood sturdily upright. This copy has sparser branches, an overly long neck, and a crooked casting. Still, who'd pass it up? $25.

Imitation Is the Highest Form of Flattertree

The bloomin' conifer in triplicate on top is a thrill to find the first time. I found one early on in my career as a forest ranger and immediately christened it the Peter Max Tree because the flourish of flowers seemed slightly psychedelic. Who knew at first sight it was actually an original Mylu design, much copied? In fact, copies date way back to near the original in the Sixties and continued to be made into the 21st Century. That's how timelessly groovy the power of flowers is as a holiday theme. On top, the centerpiece is the oldest one and, done in (now-faded) Technicolor tones, strongly suggests a favored Beatrix coloration, so we could assume all sorts of things from that. Did Beatrix by chance manufacture that particular Mylu design and then re-use it later for itself or another jewelry house? Did a middleman borrow a version of the Mylu tree and bring it to other manufacturers for other retail destinations? Or did other jewelry houses use that loud metallic *mix* of greens and reds? (I've only seen it in B.J. pins.) On right is a completely fresh version of the tree, using pastel rhinestones and creamy opaque epoxy, rendering this Christmas tree almost spring-like. It's from the Nineties. The version on far left is a bit of a bore, just gold metal and clear crystals. They are $25-50.

Down a row is another clever design tree-o, one also located early on in vintage form, and once again I was unaware it was a Mylu rip-off. Quickly dubbed the Jetsons Tree, it seemed ultramodern or futuristic. I was aghast (at myself) for plunking down $35 so fast, since at that point I was accustomed to department-store holiday jewelry only, mostly $5-15. This was pre-Internet, pre-antiques malls. The Jetsons tree was sitting temptingly in an antiques shop on Cherokee Street in St. Louis. Who could pass up this kooky confection with its eager, 'I hope you like me' tilt. The far right version (center row) is the original find, and the sun- or starburst engraving gives it an extra Outer Space effect. Multicolor stones are a nice touch, as are the pave-set brilliants in the lower perimeter and colored stones in the trunk; $50+. To its left is a newer version with pleasing greening and bigger stones; $25-50. The version on far left doesn't have the color or detailing to make it extremely compelling; $20-25.

The Mylu sisters also created the original version of the trees in the bottom row. This quartet is rather anemic and weedy looking, while the original signed versions are brawnier and less … sad. Still, there's something about merry even when it isn't tip-top. $10-25.

Xmas Textiles

One of the most unusual Christmas tree pins in our collection is a small Indian-rug brooch, but it's signed, so we'll save it for another book.

The most common and some of the oldest of all vintage tree pins are of course sequined felt (above), some as old as the Great Depression.

(The huge red heart at right is actually a small pillow, so we'll skip it and move on to pins.)

Beyond old felt, opposite top left, is a hooked-rug brooch with primitive feather tree motif in its pattern, backed with leather and utterly charming; 3 inches, $50.

Below it is a newer felt heart brooch with Christmas tree stitchery (red whip-stitches, blue pot, white on cream snowflakes) and tiny bead accents as red ornaments on needle tips; $15. The bristly old 1940s brush brooch below left is flocked and decorated with beads, all attached to a rounded wooden base; $10-25.

Pieces of antique quilts compose the twine-topped tree with thimble base wrapped in plaid fabric. It's a clever creation, buttons serving as variously-sized ornaments sewn on with very visible red threading. The antique-quilting scraps even show old stains. And as mentioned on top, twisted twine forms a bow-top finish; 3+ inches, $50

Pink netting forms the ethereal tiers of this antique arbor on bottom right, dolled up with pearlescent beads and glitter. Netting was never so big as in the Fifties, but this brooch looks even older in person. Wire shaped as scalloped tiers anchors the old girl's gauzy sails. It's 3+ inches, $25-50.

Pine Pin Potpourri III

The crazy quilt of Christmas designs here hints at the infinite variety in the vast jeweled forest. You could focus on any style or category and build a collection around it, from stripes to tree transportation.

If stripes work so well in fashion ties, no reason they wouldn't succeed in trees. Striped pines are instant classics. Remember the first time you ever saw deep blue and green combined – in plaid school uniforms or forest-green knee socks with blue wool shorts? These vintage trees hearken back to that first-impression impact. Diagonally-striped tree of metallic blue and green with rope-edged tiers manages both shine and patina; $50. Blue and green tree (middle) is a perfect beauty, with impeccable enameling and exactingly shaped, coiffured boughs; $50. Third blue-greenie (right) is a sloppier sister of the middle tree. Even snow-like polka dots don't cover up the poorer, clunkier casting; $25+ Red, cream and gold stripes on second vintage tree suggest a sailboat; $25-50. Familiar tree with addition of red-stripe garland has defined boughs and pot made merrier with simple touch of tiny red dots; $25. New golden ringer far right is something different from striped brigade, using textures to make a statement. Contrasting side shapes are clever, showing how attractive metal-only can be when used inventively; $25+

Christmas quartet of epoxied pines (second row) hale from various May Department Stores ca. early '90s. Back then, these seemed like the cat's meow and bee's knees rolled into one. The first two, in rich green or white, verge on being misshapen, one reason they're unusual. Polychrome pastes are bezel-set into trees. Translucent green epoxy allows patterned metal to show through, while ivory cream opaque epoxy covers it; $50+ each. If the next two hadn't been sold with Christmas jewelry, you'd think they were veined, jeweled leaves. Instead, they're rhapsodies on a theme, foliate-shaped Xmas arbors scattered with jewel-tone or pastel stones; $50 A silvery triangle with golden star is unremarkable, but probably related to the concoction above it; $10-20.

Who was the first wit to celebrate the annual tradition of buying or chopping a tree and hauling it home atop the auto? Well-defined golden car carrying tall green tree (how nice: it's already decorated!) is a sort of Fiat-Saab-Ghia hybrid. Clever figaro-chain straps hold tree to rooftop; $25-50. The tree transport below it, a stylized Beetle, came attached to greeting cards, stamped, soldered, makeshift concoctions with a certain humble charm; $25+

Vintage trio (center) includes a partridge tree, bell and wreath of cast metal with quilted floral and foliate pattern with ridges recalling embroidery threads; $100-150 set. Far right: marvelous design with ridiculous detail, notably the knobs on trunk of wood and bark. Pewter finish makes classic Art-color stones of orange, sapphire and topaz really pop. This baum also delights with layered casting; $75-150.

Stamped star with snowflake pattern is attached via cabochon bead to stamped tree; $10-20. An almost muddy-mint pair is familiar when bare, but the colored epoxy glue sprinkled with glitter changes look completely. $25-50 (from small shops in the Victorian village of Kimmswick, Missouri. Bottom row: Stylized geometry results in surreal ridged golden triangles encased by wide frames of pave-set RS on silver-plated metal. Trees look like Vero creations, from SteinMart; $25-50. Elaborate, layered RS-chain tree with Hobe-style curlicue was an expensive brooch at Nordstrom in 1998, reportedly by a Washington State-maker for the upscale chain; $75-150. Next to it, a similarly-themed RS brooch that was much less costly; $25. An enormous Techie Tree gaily lit for computer geeks with the Christmas spirit, winking and blinking its way onto lapels; $25-50.

Trees With Characters

An entire book could be devoted to or collection built around trees plus creatures, characters or things. The examples here make up a teensy sampling of unsigned-only pairings.

The brightly colored reindeer who resembles Bullwinkle the Moose, actually, looks a lot like an Edgar Berebi piece but is not signed. Christmas pines are used as many things but this may be the first use as ornamented antlers. An unusual novelty, $50+

Another novel use of a tree, this time as one angle of a five-point star. The tree stands out because the star is a hushed gold-plated metal while the arbor is rich green with rhinestone ornaments. This brooch is highly dimensional, making it more than an afterthought. It has real depth and is quite special in person; $50+

Top row right, the vintage wire-worked and rhinestoned tree triangle becomes a Star of David that looks like a hand-held fan, $25+

The tree with 3-D snowman was the first Guy with Tree I ever found, a vintage pin that features lightly enameled tree with snowman made of balls of glass mosaics, like specks of coconut. Eyes and mouth are painted on. His metal top hat flecked with holly leaves is part of the metal frame with tree, the snowballs attached to the frame base. Quite a special creation; $50+

Funny Santa tree goes either way, whether you want to see a tree with Kris Kringle in there somewhere or (upside down), Santa with beard. It's either painted wood or composite, the nose and mustache glued on separately; $25+

It's a mini chorus line of Christmas motifs in a vividly hued arrangement of reindeer, tree and snowman. There's something primitive and folkloric about the epoxied pin; $25

The bottom row boasts a trio of Clauses, all vintage. Father Christmas (left) in brilliant cardinal-red garb carries a pine tree to the town-square festivities, $25-50+. The center Santa with loads of gifts 'neath the tree is interesting because he is still being made today. This design turns up, brand new, out of China. Vintage version, as here, $25-50+. And of course everyone recognizes the fellow on right: a poor vintage copy of the famous Hollycraft Kringle, a tree abstraction that looks much more abstract than usual here; $25-50+

Czech List

Beautiful? Absolutely. Old? Some sellers swear so. No one took that proposition further than Horchow during Christmas 2007, when it proffered for sale one after another Christmas tree brooch Horchow stated was 'ca. 1935 Czech.' As each tree out of many designs was sold, an exact duplicate would appear in its stead in the online shop, again for sale. Sorry we didn't purchase one to show you. Each tree cost $500 to $1,000. The jewelry world went wild – since it's generally accepted among jewelry cognoscenti that the vast majority of 'Czech' trees are raw (unplated) castings being loaded with stones right now. Like many jewelry specialists, I called Horchow to talk to them about the 'vintage' or 'antique' brooches and was told someone would be in touch.

Collecting Czech is a hazy area, so it's crucial to stick to what's known. Just for starters, we know no tree with stones turned iridescent thanks to an aurora borealis film can be earlier than 1955. Further, large-size Christmas tree pins are ultra-rare when vintage, period, but we are to find credible thousands of antique Czech trees at well over 3 inches in height. (Huge trees weren't common or popular until the 1990s.) My older son spent the Christmas holidays during his junior year (2004) in Vienna and Prague and bought two Czech-style Christmas tree pins for me from shops in Wien. They were being widely sold in shops and hotels, with no advertising suggesting they were old at all. A friend also bought a new tree in Prague for me. Next, 'antique Czech trees' started turning up in great profusion several years ago in antiques malls across the country, dealers adding excited signs proclaiming rarity, with lots of exclamation points. (It was as if a new vein in a Christmas jewelry mine had been tapped in the old country.) Another conundrum: We're to believe designers from decades past, 50 to 70 years ago, chose the most beautiful stones at their disposal but decided not to gild the metal or care that ugly solder besmirched back sides while gorgeous art glass decorated the fronts. The casts are left raw to suggest age (except – sometimes – for the designer cartouche, which might be gleaming with gold plating).

Who wouldn't want to purchase a ravishing European tree for $25 to $75, no matter its age or provenance? But once you get into the $100-plus range and into the $1,000 stratosphere, collectors must know what they're getting, including unimpeachable proof of a pin's vintage.

The majority of 'Czech' trees are unsigned; the most well-known mark on Czech Christmas trees is probably Husár D, while others include Design by Jana, Design by Romi ... The trees shown here are unmarked. They appeared before 'Czech' trees turned much fancier and more elaborate. The two trees in the bottom row were *not* billed as Czech, but are included to show how similar they are in shape and nature to Czech trees. I bought them in Manhattan shops in 1998-99, the one on bottom left because at that point I had never seen khaki stones in a tree before. Either of these, if left unplated, could double as a putative Czech pine; $25. All the others were either advertised as Czech or purchased in Austria or the Czech Republic, are unplated – and some have solder dust in the crevices of the rhinestone chain; $50+ I'm personally partial to primitive-looking pines, and many of the trees have dazzling crystals, creamy cabochons or, better yet, a mix of both, so it's a shame so many have been scared off the Czech deck, afraid of a wreck.

Mixed Metals

Silvers warmed by copper, gold and bronze chilled by argent ... ah, the joys of mixed metals in Christmas tree pins.

The oldest mix might be in Art-signed trees, that year they did all-metal versions of their designs rather than their piney-greens and creamy-snow enamels with blue and orange rhinestones.

The most frequently done arrangement of mixed metals over the past few decades has been in stamped collage pieces, simply because it's so easy to pick and choose and match one color here, another there.

The tree on top right is a perfect example of this technique: a brass base that's a sort of rounded triangle has a single, large golden tree glued onto it. The tree is enameled for snow effect, has two golden winged angels flanking its sides and holding a garland of rhinestone chain between them, while a tiny cherub tops the tannenbaum. Two smaller snowy pines further flank the angels, and running across the base are poinsettias, one a darker gold, two silver outlined in gold; $25.

Opposite the angel trees, in the second row (left), is another version of collage. All of the pieces are separate, from trunks to stars, for full differentiation. On left is an antiqued silver tree with wave pattern body, beam-patterned star hosting emerald stone, and a plain silver trunk. The brass tree in center of collage is taller, has a simpler pattern, and its oversized star looks so different with a ruby cabochon. The smaller copper tree on right has an arts-and-crafts pattern and a pinwheel star; $25. Many collage pieces are signed, and they'll be shown in another book.

The tree on top (left) is a layered cast piece that might look right as an arbor Ichabod Crane gallops by during a midnight ride. The weighty construction is unusual, with open, recessed area built into the bronze base, having protruding ornament nubs onto which fits an antiqued-silver metal tree with holes. $25-50

The second row on right appears to be a triple casting of trees, but is actually a cast collage. Each tree is cast, but then glued together, the copper tree in the middle actually much larger than the bronze and silver, thus able to anchor them. Mixed-metal colors and varying patterns (petals, curlicues, stars) heighten the color difference. $25

The large (almost 4 inches) tree on bottom sometimes turns up with a Mexico stamp, but this one is unmarked in any way. Incorporating three different metal shades in its showy self, the delicate golden candy canes are slender and appear more fragile because they stand up away from the tree. The aluminum-like silver metal is reflective. $25+ More wearable than collectible, it causes pangs every time I see it, the sole tree remaining from a large collection snapped up before I arrived at the Eureka Antiques Mall. Blast!

Patreeotics

The Sept. 11 attacks on the World Trade Center turned the classic Christmas colors of red and green to red, white and blue in 2001 and 2002. The 2001 pins had to be made quickly to cash in on sentiment for all things American and patriotic, while there was much more time to manufacture flag-topped and flag-draped Christmas trees for the 2002 season, when patriotic passions remained stirred. While vintage trees capturing Old Glory do exist, the biggest patriotic pin surge was born out of 9-11's tragic aftermath.

The host of holiday flags cleverly masquerading as Christmas pins here represent a smattering of unsigned trees signifying a political fervor unfamiliar to many Americans who had not lived through World War II. That global conflict spawned a great quantity of imaginative jewelry, the money its sales raised often used toward the war effort. Political and patriotic jewelry has a long history in America, noting happy occasions such as Centennials, the end of war or the Moon Landing, to sad, from Pearl Harbor to the assassination of President John F. Kennedy.

The patriotic holiday pines here sum up the three basic motifs that were made. In one group, past tree designs were updated with American flags planted into treetops. Ironically, most of these were made in China, not America. The second category, more artistic and imaginative, incorporates the patterns and colors of the flag into the tree design. On top right, the creamy white stripes combined with translucent red and opaque navy are particularly attractive against silver-plated metal, the tiered stripes studded with ruby and sapphire cabochons. The third niche in patriotics is the subtlest, jeweled trees simply decorated in a riot of blue and red rhinestones.

The small wooden tree on lower left is the oldest here, the plastic novelty on bottom the cheapest. They are of course collectible, as keepsakes or *souvenirs tristes* of a country's dark day, to be worn in subsequent years as patriotic mementos eventually relieved of their complete affiliation with mourning.

Mirror Images

The Christmas tree pins on the opposite page illustrate several things. One, vintage trees identical to pricey signed trees are plentiful and sell for a lot less. Two, knockoffs galore exist of successful designs, some good, some not so much. Three, some designs are copied and manufactured long after the original design was made.

The entire top row (plus the pin in middle of second row) are all twins or close doubles of the signed Weiss circus clown tree, like big, polka-dotted collars. This design always bewitches a collector at first sight and few collections don't feature one. The center top tree with big blue and yellow crystals and aurora-borealis ruby stones is the classic, but the addition of an enamel whitewash makes it even better than the standard gold finish. The other three have more rhinestone polka dots and also enjoy extras from whitewash, greenwash, and faux pearls on the scalloped edge of one. What can you say other than it's a terrific tree design with scads of examples out there; $25-50+

At either end of the second row are two skeletal vintage copies of the great Warner chandelier Christmas pin. The real thing is one of the loveliest, most delicate and refined pines ever made, so someone thought they should get in on the brilliant execution ... but didn't quite achieve lift-off. These two aren't without their vintage charms, and the oversized sparkler atop the sample on right is a fun touch, but these scrawny saplings lack the impact of the exquisitely made originals; $25+

The bottom row center shows another copy of a great Warner tree. This one is well-cast and has the bonus of garish metallic touches – royal blue ornaments, green-tipped branches, red and gold gifts – but again doesn't match the elegance of the signed-Warner original, one of the great beauties.

The most puzzling aspect of those two lacy tannenbaum at either end (below) is that one of them appears to be older than the actual signed version of this design, marked Sweet Romance. Was this an unsigned vintage creation adopted by that company, perhaps? This is another of the all-time great Christmas tree pins, a mass of webbed filigree in a pattern that can be seen as snowflakes, flora or spider webs, dressed up with polychrome paste. Hard to say which is prettier, the pastel version or the jazzy jewel tones, but certainly the large square-cut stone in the tree trunks are a perfect finishing touch. $25-50+

The Resin for the Season

Next Christmas, don't make cookies, cast your own homemade resin brooches. While not as easy as baking gingerbread, how fun to crank out your own Christmas tree pins with a wide range of effects, from ivory-like to glass-like, depending on the resin you use. It's a versatile medium for jewelry. For instance, after making a silicon mould from a favorite Christmas tree ornament, turn it into a brooch and transform it with paints or translucent acrylic resin. The molds may be rigid (metal, wood, plaster, fiberglass) or flexible (silicon or polysulfides). Pour the liquid resin in to cast the shape. Resin options include acrylics, polyesters and epoxies.

The crazy cast of Christmas pins on the next page could not be called elegant or beautiful, but they exhibit a primitive sense of juvenile whimsy. It might be more fun to build a mini-art gallery of these resin sculptures for the holidays than wear them.

Santa top left is either stuck in a chimney or ringing a bell for The Salvation Army. Amazing how much work goes into these almost-always cheap resin pins. In this case, the main piece was cast and painted, a separate tree set *en tremblant* in front, and trembler bell added as an accessory; $10-25. Next is a Yuletide line-up of bell, Kris Kringle, Christmas tree and gift-filled sleigh, all forming a large barrette-turned-brooch; $10-25.

Old-fashioned Father Christmas fellows in second row are notable for wood-like effect; $10-25. If you like true novelties, you won't find many boxer trees in jewelry land, and this springy sapling even has boxing gloves loaded onto two of four appendages; $10-25. If you find children or animals dressed as trees irresistible, the cutie on the right has the look of a Precious Moments product, with a Teddy tossed casually into the mix; $10-25.

The star of the third row is on right, Santa fishing for his trout, er, tree, a spring-loaded line employed for ice fishing on a frozen North Pole pond; $15-30. The other two Santa-plus-tree pins are notable for a clinging Santa who is hiding and worried, and a Santa who is virtually verklempt about Noel, another barrette-turned-brooch; $10-20. Hey, Santa, your face is gonna *freeze* like that.

In the bottom row are some huge hunks of burnin' resin, suitable for winter coats. Clauszilla proffers a pine, $25. A sloganizing snowman (Let It Snow) has his hands full, so all the resin charms are left dangling below, $10-25. A white-bearded bearer of gifts holds a green tree up against his snowy *barbe*, $10-25. And a red-bowed creature (is it a cat or dog?) cozies up under the tannenbaum with a gift, a gingerbread boy smooshed temptingly nearby; $15-30.

We Wish You a Crafty Christmas

This conglomeration of Christmas creations only goes to show how many ways there are to trim a tree.

Some may not have begun their lives as holiday arbors, but grew into the role with considerable panache. Random acquisitions, they may not have a lot of story behind them, but are illustrative of variety and imagination and also have rarity going for them.

The quirky forest includes metal with stones, plastic-coated composition, thin metal puzzle pieces, lacquered plastics, and rhinestone chain on wood.

Left to right, top: Unusual arbor with oversized jewel, probably born an earring, converted to pin, $25; plastic, mixed-pattern teepee tree in shades of gold and black, missing its star, $25+; Graffiti tree (right) with star-shaped hole was the favorite in the entire book of one of my children, so that rates a $50+.

Second row, left: a sort of puzzle-pieces tree of metal and coated cardboard, similar to bottom-row middle tree, the top one static, the lower tree articulated, dangling and swingy, $30-50 each.

Bottom left is a dressy, black-metal tree with imbedded rhinestones and showy RS star, $50. On right, a wooden tree with very old, applied rhinestone chain and the same style star as on left black, so clearly made by the same artist; $50.

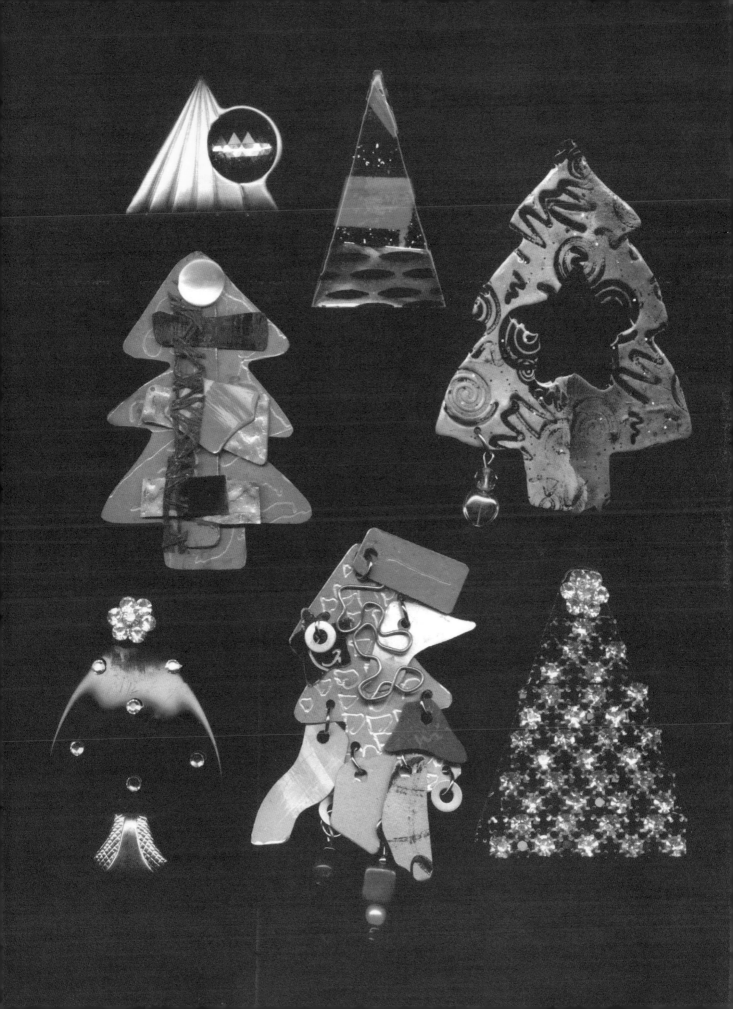

White Christmas

Snow-white enameled gold-plated tree (top) is Warholian, features a Campbell's Soup can ; $50.

The angel-topped trees with snowflake ornamentation may be found in both vintage and newer permutations. Vintage versions are heavy and cast; newer angel trees are stamped. In the late 1990s and early 2000s, these seemed almost ubiquitous, although the vintage cast piece is harder to locate. Under the angel trees is a star tree of glittered opaque white epoxy that is a duplicate to a signed Kirks Folly design, but this is an unsigned twin probably made in China; $10.

Flanking the stars tree are two plainspoken pines very Jonette- or Gerry-like, but unmarked, one with multicolor chaton, $10-20, and one with painted metallic-purple knobs; $10-20.

At base page is one of the all-time great unsigned trees, a lattice-work confection that looks like cracked ice on a window, decorated with polychrome cabochons in edged bezels. A brilliant vintage design, $75-150.

Holiday Sparklers

Karl Eisenberg remarked, as we looked at one of the company's Christmas tree pins, that consumers didn't realize how much more work went into brooches of soldered rhinestone chain – versus cast pieces. So you can think about that when you see the dizzying array of rhinestone-chain pins in the enormous Christmas category. They are legion. Granted, not so many are highly collectible, but instead, merry little sparklers perfect to mass together on a lapel. Every collector requires the pin that says 'I Love Trees' with a heart symbol for love and a rhinestone pine for the Christmas arbor. Most lean toward a preference for crystal, red and green rhinestones, some add candle accents or jingle bells. The choice is vast, and they are so reasonably priced, it's frequently where beginning collectors … begin. $10-25

The Trees of 2007

Quick shops, gas stations, discount stores, national fashion franchises and even Dollar Tree (appropriately) are venues where savvy jewelry sleuths dig up Christmas tree pins. Walgreens used to carry unique oddball holiday pins but in 2007 went with cheap, unimaginative cast-metal pins that have been done to death in much better style. Oh, well. The stellar group here represents a smattering of unsigned saplings shop-and-chopped during holidays '07. The silver-loops tree with rhinestone dangles, as well as the candle-like tree with flame star and the banana-branch tree next to it all sprang up at Value City, with original retail prices of $16.99 each. (Kudos, VCity, for attempting a modicum of creativity, unlike much swankier museum shops, which keep cranking out the same boring trees year after year.) The snowy flakes tree on top is a confection from Target, and has tons of seasonal appeal. To the right of snowflakes is a pagoda-influenced pine found at Kohl's, while the other Asian-accented arbor, on the left, is refined sterling, marcasite and crystals from T.J. Maxx, $29.99. The festive little emeralds tree brooch is a honey from Sears, and the red and white layered parfait came from Dollar Tree. Let's see, how much did it cost? ;) The quilty Christmas tree with stripes and checks patterned boughs boasts tinseled tiers. It's from Kohl's, as is the penguin pile-up on right. The light-bulb'd penguin pine (enameled metal versus the resin on right) is from an old Christmas tree pins stalwart, SteinMart, which used to have an exceptional array of arbors, but has gone rapidly down hill on that front. (This one's adorable, but SteinMart used to carry 25 other designs equally as appealing.) Not much of any excitement graced Macy's, and its trees from last year turned up this year for $20 less each at the Chinese wholesale shops. Of course, many other saps of '07 aren't showcased here because they were signed (see them in an upcoming book). And we don't intend to infer here that high-end emporia don't carry swell unsigned pines. They do, but this year, the ones we saw at Saks, Neiman-Marcus and Nordstrom were marked and identified.

Hanna Bernhard
Xmas tree pins
$400-$1000

Hanna Bernhard Paris

on French-bakelite.com

Our son Samuel
for
Hanna Bernhard